INTELLECTUAL EMERGENCIES:
Some Reflections on Mothering and Teaching and a Family Album CD

Lilian G. Katz, PhD • Stephen J. Katz

Published Exclusively by KPress, a division of Kaplan Early Learning Company

P.O. Box 67
Lewisville, NC 27023
800-334-2014
www.kaplanco.com

Product code# 16807
ISBN#978-0-88076-688-3

Intellectual Emergencies, A Family Album CD, All songs © Stephen J. Katz
 Stephen is composer and performer of tracks 1-11 except where indicated.
Tracks 1, 4 and 8 appear on First Person Singular.
Tracks 7 and 10 appear on Looking Up.
Tracks 12 and 13 were composed, performed, and recorded by Miriam and Bill Millikin.

Production Team
Edited by Keith L. Pentz
Cover Design, CD Design and Layout Design by Kelly R. Andrus
Director of Publishing, Pat Conte

Printed in the United States of America

Table of Contents

Preface

Over a period of many years of teaching and conducting workshops for teachers, parents, and students all over the world, I have used the principles that arose from what I always thought as something like "intellectual emergencies" my younger son Stephen put me through from about the age of five throughout his growing years. Frequently, following my presentations to many educators over a period of some forty years in which I have referred to the principles and described the "emergencies" from which they emerged, I have been asked to make the stories and their associated principles available in print. The preparation of this booklet began in response to such requests.

As the work of putting together the twelve principles proceeded, I requested of Steve that he include in this work some of the songs he wrote, especially those related to his reflections on his own growth and experience of our family life. The songs are based on his own lyrics and are performed by him. He tells his stories of how they came to be written in Part V. I also invited Stephen's brother Dan, and his sister Miriam, to comment on the work in progress in any way they wished. As my conversations with them proceeded, we decided to add a few items of theirs that expanded this book into more of a family memoir. Their contributions in Part VI at the end of this collection illustrate clearly their characteristic humor and exceptional abilities to play with words that they shared with Stephen, as well as their exceptional abilities to make puns they inherited from their father, Boris. A few of their pieces are included in the last part of the book along with some family photographs. The inclusion of their pieces helps to put the stories of my experience as a young mother into a broader context.

I also decided to add two other items to the set of papers in this collection because they are not generally available elsewhere. Part III consists of what I call "The Last Class Notes." Early in my career as an instructor of graduate courses in which most of the students were teachers of young children, I took the opportunity at the last class meeting to summarize some main ideas and thoughts. This became an end-of-semester habit, and gradually over the years the notes grew longer and longer so that there were finally twenty-one "notes" on the list. As readers will see, some of the notes on this list are related to the principles that came from the *intellectual emergencies* and are discussed in greater detail in Part II.

As we complete this collection, Dan is fifty-three years old, and the father of fifteen-year-old twin sons. Stephen, age fifty-two, is the father of nearly three-year-old Olin. My daughter Miriam, now fifty-one years old, is the mother of three teenagers, two sons and a daughter. Sadly, my husband, Boris - their wonderful father and grandfather - passed away in 2005, leaving all of us with rich and warm memories of deep love and constant support, as well as much humor. We all miss him, and we always will.

Intellectual Emergencies and Related Principles

Part I. Introduction

There was a time when our three children were ages one, two, and three. I recall that in those days and sometimes long nights, I felt as though they were plugged into me, and my batteries were constantly running low. My husband, Boris, was a very involved and supportive father from the start. But, of course, he was away at work during those hours of the day when the children were most lively.

During those early years we lived in a small house in the shadow of the Cow Palace at the southern edge of the city of San Francisco. It never occurred to me at that time that I would ever have a job or, for any other reason, would not be taking full time care of my three energetic children. The highlight of my weekdays was an excursion to the nearby supermarket with all three children in tow. That way, at least, I got out of the noisy little house a few times a week. On one such occasion I met a neighborhood acquaintance who told me about a nearby parent cooperative nursery school that welcomed three-year-olds. Within a week our eldest child, three-year-old Dan, was enrolled in the Visitacion Valley Parent Cooperative Nursery School; and so was I.

At that time, the parent co-ops, as they were called in 1957, required parents' involvement in two ways. One was to serve as an assistant to the head teacher one morning a week in one's own child's class; the other involvement was to attend a parent education class one evening a week. Because her main responsibilities were to educate the parents, the director of the cooperative nursery school was employed by the adult education division of the local school district. The director also had the responsibility of running the daily preschool sessions that were housed in the local community center.

As I recall, the parents also paid a small enrollment fee that helped to cover the expenses of the daily program for the children.

The weekly evening classes addressed issues and topics that were designed to help us in our roles as parents of preschoolers as well as in our roles as assistant teachers in the preschool classes. In addition, parents were strongly encouraged to contribute to the management and operation of the nursery school, of which they were essentially the owners.

These experiences in the parent education classes led me to new ways of feeling and thinking about my own childhood, about my own three children, and about my own role as a parent. These classes also stimulated my interest in young children's development and the nature of parenting in general, about early childhood pedagogy, and specifically about the field of nursery education. Five years of involvement in three successive parent cooperatives as we moved away from the city of San Francisco to the suburbs, deepened my awareness of how profoundly interesting children are. Much was also to be learned from observing them, from knowing them as well as knowing about them, and from interacting with them, as well as learning about the wide variety of ways adults can support them.

I had completed two years as an undergraduate at Whittier College in southern California before I met my husband in San Francisco. We married the following November. I then continued my undergraduate studies at San Francisco State College, taking courses in three languages, political science, economics, literature and other topics of interest, until the birth of our first child, Dan. Within two-and-a-half years, Dan was joined by Stephen and Miriam. However, until that time I had not completed a bachelor's degree, partly because I had not quite understood the system of collecting required credits needed to complete a degree, and partly because it had not occurred to me that I would ever need a degree, or ever have a job.

When our youngest child, Miriam, moved on to the kindergarten, I accepted a position as a teacher of the three-year-old class at the Redwood Parents' Cooperative Nursery School in nearby Redwood City, California. At that time, no formal state qualifications were required for such a position. At the same time, I registered for an evening class on child development and early education at nearby San Mateo Community College, a class taught by Dr. Mary B. Lane. Dr. Lane was also full time Professor of Education at San Francisco State College. While I was a student in her community college class she urged me to complete my bachelor's degree so that I could plan a career as a qualified teacher. I discovered then that I only needed one class in a science to complete the required credits for the bachelor's degree, and completed it in 1964.

In the meantime, as I continued to teach at Redwood Parents' Nursery School and began to realize that I needed more formal training in nursery teaching methods. The closest university to our home that had a nursery school on campus was Stanford University. With the invaluable assistance of Dr. Lane, I was able to meet Professor Pauline Sears at Stanford. All I had hoped for was to be admitted into a class on nursery teaching methods. However, following a very long discussion with Prof. Sears, she invited me to become a graduate student, offered me a scholarship, and said, "Finish up your bachelor's degree and start here at Stanford in the spring quarter. But we have no Master's program here. You'll have to do a PhD." So, that is how I was launched into a very satisfying career in the field of early childhood education.

As to our three children, they are alike in many ways. As I have already indicated, all three are loving, creative, imaginative, and humorous, as can be seen in their contributions included in Part VI of this book. All three are now themselves devoted parents. They are also of course, unique in many ways. Of special relevance to this book is the particular way in which our middle one, Steve, from about the age of five, repeatedly challenged my requests, demands, views, assertions and assumptions, and thereby provoked me to think them through, to explain my positions, and often to justify them. He seemed always determined to make up his own reflective mind about matters at hand – usually after considerable thought. Steve was also very ready and willing to share with me his reflections and re-analyses of various events in his life. In this way, from very early on Steve presented me with what I came to think of as *intellec-*

tual emergencies: moments when I felt that I had to make up something in a hurry with which to respond to his queries and challenges.

This first part of the book presents some dozen or so of the main principles that emerged from such *intellectual emergencies* encountered with Steve over the years of his growth and early maturity. I have included those principles that were especially useful to my own teaching and learning and that I have shared with students and colleagues for many years.

In 1968 upon completion of my PhD at Stanford University our family moved from northern California to central Illinois where I joined the faculty at the University of Illinois. The children were then eleven, twelve, and thirteen-years old – not an easy time in their lives for children to move. Soon after we settled in Champaign-Urbana my husband undertook graduate work in urban planning. Our plan at the time was to return to California when his graduate studies were completed. However, we never again seriously considered returning to California.

Over a period of more than forty years, my work in the field of early childhood education has included teaching primarily graduate courses in the field, both on and off campus, as well as presenting seminars, workshops, and lectures in all fifty US states and more than fifty other countries. I also served as the Director of the ERIC Clearinghouse on Elementary & Early Childhood Education for 33 years, until the national ERIC system was closed down in 2003.

I have told the stories of these incidents with Steve to help put ideas and principles into their real context and to clarify various aspects of their application. While the principles drawn from these predicaments are particularly relevant to teaching young children, some of them apply also to teaching in general, and some to parenting in particular. I invited Steve to share contemporary reflections on experiences described, and he indicated that they certainly brought back memories, but that he had nothing further to add to them.

The set of principles that follows is offered in order of their generality rather than in the chronological order in which the particular *intellectual emergencies* occurred. For example, the first principle on the list (for which I have been unable to find a catchy or simple term) seems to me to apply to all teaching, of all subjects, of all age groups of learners; whereas most of the other principles are more relevant to parenting and teaching younger children.

The term principle is used here to refer to a generalization that is sufficiently reliable, that it is worthy of consideration when trying to make a choice from among possible alternatives concerning what actions to take, or in some cases, not to take. As such, principles are like decision rules in that they help to guide choices from among a range of possible courses of action. The principles are not laws of behavior that are always true, to be applied mindlessly, but are intended to be qualified by such phrases as "under most similar circumstances," or "in situations like these." A decision rule that is always true or right or appropriate under all conditions would be referred to as a "law." (Katz & Raths, 1992) Unfortunately, in child rearing and in teaching, such "laws" have not yet been uncovered, at least, not to my knowledge. Both roles – parenting and teaching - are filled with ambiguities and uncertainties even though our children are more likely to feel supported by parents and teachers who convey at least an optimal level of confidence in what they are proposing or demanding. This inherent uncertainty is most likely characteristic of all roles in the helping professions. Conducting the kinds of double-blind random assignment experiments that would include placebos that are required for certainty of the findings would be unethical in our fields. In such cases, our best option for deepening and improving our practices is to share our ideas and thinking openly with our colleagues and engage in frequent discussion, argument and debate.

In addition to their potential usefulness, we hope that the discussion of these principles will also encourage readers to formulate their own principles, drawing on their own *intellectual emergencies* with their own children as well as those whom they teach.

This book also includes a compact disc recording of Steve's performance of some of the songs he composed over a period of many years. The disc includes primarily those songs that are related to his growing years and his reflections of various family experiences. Steve is the singer of all songs as well as guitarist, cellist and drummer in many of them. In Part V Steve describes the backgrounds and events that provoked the creation of the lyrics and the composition of the songs and some other details to help us appreciate more fully the songs that are included.

Part II. Principles of Teaching

Principle No. 1. Teach the Learners How to Tell You Where They Are.

As Steve gradually and, at times, somewhat reluctantly made his way through his undergraduate and master's degree studies in music, primarily studying the cello, my husband and I kept our fingers crossed that he would ultimately find some kind of satisfying as well as remunerative employment. We worried about how many professional cellists the world really needs compared to the number available. We were not very optimistic about his prospects and we regretted that we had not encouraged him to regard his cello playing as something to enjoy primarily on the weekends.

After completing his master's degree in cello at the Conservatory of Music in Cincinnati, Steve joined the newly formed Essex quartet headquartered in Connecticut. During that period he spent some time with the Tokyo Quartet at Yale University. His father and I still kept hoping that something more reliable and financially rewarding for him would turn up. Then late one evening early in the summer of 1988 Steve telephoned to tell us that he had accepted a position as a teacher of cello at The Connecticut Conservatory of Dance and Music in New Milford, Connecticut. We were so relieved when we got this news. At last, we thought, he would have a regular, even if low, income! After we chatted about the arrangements for his new job and some of the details of the post, I told Steve that I was just about to leave for a lecture tour in New Zealand for a couple of weeks, and that while traveling I would write to him a series of letters outlining my current thinking about what I had come to think of as some main principles of teaching. This offer was not out of line with many discussions Steve and I had enjoyed over the years about his school experiences, and about my work.

Since about the age of twelve, Steve had often expressed interest in my work. From time to time, he would ask me, "What are you making up these days?" On those occasions I gladly shared with him whatever I was working on, or thinking, or reading, or writing about that might be of interest to him. Invariably his reactions to my responses to his question were thoughtful and pertinent. He showed genuine interest in what I said and occasionally offered some additions or suggestions about the ideas I shared with him. Thus, my promise to write to him about the principles of teaching – a topic I was quite involved in for several years - was consistent with our relationship at that time. His response to my promise of letters about the principles of teaching was, "Great! That's just what I'm gonna need!"

I then departed on my lecture tour. I enjoyed a few weeks of hopping around the two beautiful islands of New Zealand, meeting wonderful colleagues there, making new friends, giving talks, visiting preschool programs and colleges and learning a great deal. I was able to visit many preschool provisions in many cities and towns and was greatly impressed by their high quality. But, with all that was going on during the trip, I did not write the promised letters to Steve. In part that was because the tour kept me very busy and exhausted, but also in part because I realized that I knew nothing about teaching a musical instrument.

I studied the violin from the age of eight until I came to the United States at the age of fifteen. Some of that study was with my mother who was a very talented violinist and had herself been something of a child prodigy. She certainly made it clear to me early on that I would have to make my way in the world by some other means – though I still love to (try to) play the fiddle! In fact, when I introduced my future husband to my mother and indicated that he was a wonderful pianist and that we were playing sonatas together, she pointed out that I was lucky that "love is not only blind, but also deaf!" For more than fifty years my husband and I played chamber music together, and that seemed to prove her point!

I returned from my New Zealand travels that summer and resumed the usual schedule of work at the University of Illinois, at that time as Director of the ERIC Clearinghouse on Elementary and Early Childhood Education, working also with doctoral students, and teaching graduate courses when the semester began. From time to time I chatted with Steve on the phone about his new post, his new living quarters, whether he would have health insurance or needed snow tires, and other matters related to his new life in Connecticut. Even after he had started teaching, our phone conversations stayed with the more mundane topics of how he was managing his new living conditions. However, we did not get into discussions of his actual work as a teacher. I never doubted that he would be a good teacher. He seemed to me to have a real knack for understanding how others think and how things look to others from their point of view. These abilities seemed to me very basic to effective teaching.

Then, late one night towards the end of October the phone rang and I picked it up to hear Steve say, "Mom, you've got to give me those letters on the phone." He was clearly referring to the letters I had earlier promised to write to him about the principles of teaching. "Why Steve?" I asked. "What's the problem?" His response was "There's so much I don't know about teaching!" To which I replied, "You can't begin as a veteran." This response on my part was based on my long experience of living with Steve who said, for example, when he was in the first grade [in those days that's when children started learning to read], "I don't want to learn how to read. I want to know how to read." So again he seemed to be saying, "I don't want to learn how to teach. I want to know how to teach." While his wish was understandable, it was not really possible. No one can begin any occupation – whether as a senator, a banker, or a mail carrier, as a veteran.

On subsequent reflection, I admit that my response was an error - probably one I would not have made if he had been one of my graduate students. But he was not my student; he was my younger son! I refer to the response as an error because, while it was a true statement, it was not a helpful one. Surely one of the important principles of teaching is to respond to students in ways that are helpful,

&

which sometimes means withholding the truth or postponing telling it until the right time or at least, a better time!

Steve's response to my "truth" was, "Well, the least you could do is to give me the first principle of teaching." There was the classic *intellectual emergency* that Steve had so frequently put me in ever since he learned to talk - challenging situations in which I felt I had to make up something in a hurry. I had not previously thought about what might be the "first" principle of teaching, though I had certainly thought much about basic principles of teaching. But which of them came first was not on my list of things to worry about. So, to respond to Steve, I had to make up something in a hurry.

I then said to Steve, "I'm not sure if this is the first or second or third principle. But it surely is among the important ones, and that is: teach the learner how to tell you where he or she is. So, for example, for someone in my field working with young children I think it is important to teach the children how to say things to the teacher like, "Hold it! I'm lost!" or "Could you show me one more time, please?" or "Could you go over that again slowly, please?" Or, perhaps, "Could you say that one more time?" Or, "Could you tell me that again with other words, please?" These similar requests indicate to the teacher where the learner is, or is not, or what parts of an explanation are not clear enough – at least for that particular learner. The main point here being that the learner can let the teacher know when and where help is needed. And, as the learner matures he or she can let the teacher know what specific kind of help is being sought.

When I finished my emergency "lecture" it was silent on the other end of the phone and I felt sure Steve had fallen asleep. So I said, "Steve, are you still there?" To which he replied in his usual thoughtful way, "Why didn't somebody say that to me when I was in second grade?" After another pause, he said, "My life in school would have been totally different if I could just have said, "Hold it! I'm lost!" Or, "Could you say that one more time, please?" He repeated the ways I had suggested that he could have let the teacher know what kind of help he needed.

Steve then said that what he remembered of his early school years was that teachers said things like, "You'd better pay attention. I'm not going over this again." Or, "You'd better listen up. I'm only going to say this once." Why would any teacher think that a group of some twenty or more children would all understand something worth teaching when it is explained only once? It is so unlikely that a group of individuals who are often (if not usually) diverse in background, culture, experience, ability, and in many other ways will all achieve understanding of something worth learning about when it is presented once and in only one way. Teachers are more likely to be effective if they ask questions of a "help-seeking" child such as, "Which part of the problem is confusing?" or "Is it this step in the problem that's not clear enough?"

As a result of this particular "emergency" call from Steve, I consistently urged my students as well as participants in the countless seminars I have conducted, and audiences that I have addressed around the world, to be sure to raise their hands and to say to me as their teacher, lecturer or speaker, "Hold it! Could you go over that again?" or "Could you give us an example of what you are suggesting?", or use another way to indicate to me what kind of help I could give them as their teacher or lecturer. When the listeners and participants in a seminar, or the students in a class know that their requests for help (i.e., further explanations and examples) are expected and welcomed, they are more likely to request them. In this way the possibility increases that all, or at least most participants will master the information and ideas being offered.

Even preschool children can learn early that their desire to understand something more fully or more clearly can be expressed in a variety of useful ways. From time to time when a teacher is suggesting an activity, or a strategy for completing a particular task or process, she or he can say, in a matter-of-fact way, something like, "If you want more help (or more explanations, etc.), just let me know. I'll be over there. I'll help you as soon as I can." I emphasize making such statements in a matter-of-fact tone so that even very young children understand that asking for further assistance or explanations or repetition of instructions should be a normal and natural part of life in the classroom.

I would like to add here that one of the many benefits of mixed-age grouping in the early years – probably up until the age of about eight years – is the way older children can respond to young ones' requests for help of various kinds. But at the same time it is important for teachers to teach the older children to say to younger ones who are seeking their help, again, in a matter-of-fact tone, something like, "I can't help you right now 'cause I'm busy. But as soon as I have finished with this I'll see what I can do to help." This kind of "help-seeking" and "help-giving" thus can become part of the culture of the class (and hopefully of the school) so that when the younger ones become, in their turn the older ones, they will respond to these situations naturally. Such "help-giving" should become part of the culture of the classroom and of the school.

On reflection, I realized that this principle had first come to mind many years before this particular phone conversation with Steve. It was provoked originally when I was observing a mathematics teacher in a class of fourteen-year-old boys in another country. The teacher was conducting a formal lesson of what seemed to me to be a clear set of instructions on how to calculate compound interest. Using the blackboard, he showed the boys several clear examples of the processes involved, and then gave them some problems to solve individually at their desks for the next fifteen or twenty minutes. Within five minutes one youngster, looking somewhat puzzled, came forward to the teacher with his exercise book open, and trying to show his work to the teacher, he said, "I'm not sure about what I've done. Have I got this right?" The teacher's response was, "I already explained how to do this. I'm not going over it again. You should have been paying attention." The boy returned to his seat slowly and quietly. As an outside visitor, it was difficult to know how to interpret what I had just observed. Was the teacher responding to this incident as one of many in a pattern of behavior of this particular boy? If so, that would be quite different in effect from responding this way to the boy if it had been the first time he had ever shown the courage to ask for help. Was the teacher's response related to a strong cultural tradition of the teacher exercising strong authority and control at all times? Could it have been the case that the teacher's response was related to the fact that an overseas visitor was observing in the back of the room, and he was assuming that his response to the boy was what the observer would have expected?

It is not only risky, but also difficult to interpret a teacher's behavior in a given incident when you are ignorant of the history of their relationships, and of the larger social and cultural context in which the particular events are occurring. The observed teacher gave instructions and directions competently. He clearly knew his subject; but he failed to interact in ways from which the youngster seeking help could have benefited. I would not have been surprised if perhaps another dozen of the boys in that class would have liked to have more help. But I could not be sure. A related principle here is *when visiting another's classroom and observing the events in progress, suspend judgment of them*, at least until the major determinants of the larger context can be learned.

While part of teaching is giving instructions and directions and telling learners what the teacher or those authorities who determine the standards and benchmarks want them to know and understand, teaching is largely interactive in nature. Even when the teacher or lecturer says things like, "I'm sure you've had the experience of X, or tried to help a child like Y," the teacher/lecturer is provoking the learner to bring his or her own experience into the moment and is in a sense interacting with the listeners and their experience.

This principle is placed at the beginning of our list because our experience as teachers convinces us that effectiveness depends so largely not just on knowing about the learner, but also knowing the learner; surely these two features of teacher-learner relationships are intertwined; but they are different in ways that are not easy to describe, yet worth seeking. One can know a lot about a child without even having met him or her; but effective teaching seems to require knowing the child personally and well, and thereby being able to interpret his or her behavior and make good decisions about the best ways to be helpful.

Principle No. 2. Life is a Series of Choices of Which Errors We Prefer

As I talked to Steve, and offered the principle outlined above, a second principle seemed to be called for, the one I have come to refer to as the *principle of choice of errors*, or, as I have more recently expressed it: *life is a series of choices of which errors we prefer*! Specifically, in terms of the importance of teaching learners to let us know that they need help, and what specific help they need, there is the potential error that some children will abuse it and ask for help when they really do not need it. Very likely there are a few children who will demand help just to get attention, or to attract or divert the attention of their peers, or because they lack the motivation to attempt to solve problems by themselves, to keep trying, or to ask classmates for help. Such children, then, might respond to the teacher's invitation to seek assistance by doing so excessively or unnecessarily. On the other hand, if as teachers we make the error of neglecting to encourage learners to feel comfortable about letting us know when and what kind of help they need, they may feel lost. Children who frequently experience the feeling of being lost and confused may attribute that experience to their own incompetence and inadequacies and, eventually give up trying to learn what is being taught or are likely to abandon attempts to make sense of what is being explained and other school matters. Since we cannot have it both ways, we have to choose the "least worst error." In this case, the "least worst error" is probably to reassure children that we want them to let us know when they feel or think that they need help. With experience we will learn to determine which children are likely to abuse the invitation to seek help, and do our best to help them meet their social needs in different ways.

Along similar and related lines is recent research on the help-seeking behavior of children in grades 3 to 6. In this study, Marchand and Skinner (2007) made a distinction between help-seeking and concealment of the need for help. Their findings suggest that children with a reasonable level of confidence in their abilities were more likely to seek help from their teachers than the low confidence children did and thus increase their level of confidence; whereas, children with low confidence in their abilities were more likely to conceal their difficulties and not to seek help and thereby increase their sense of incompetence which in turn increased their conceal-ment in a negative cycle, as the authors suggest:

> Analyses of reciprocal effects of students' help-seeking and conceal-ment on changes in teacher support corroborated hypothesized cycles in which motivationally "rich" children, by constructively seeking help become "richer", whereas motivationally "poor" children, by conceal-ing their difficulties, become "poorer." Age differences in children's motivational resources across the transition to middle school paralleled age differences in help-seeking and concealment (Marchand & Skin-ner, 2007, p. 65)

Children who are caught in negative cycles cannot break these cycles by themselves; they require the help of adults to do so. Breaking the negative cycle is fairly easy to do during the early years; but if we wait until the children are six- or seven-years old, and older, it becomes a much more difficult challenge. For example, by age ten or twelve, a child will have accumulated at least a half-a-dozen years of clear and convincing evidence inside him/herself that he/she is incompetent. Being "nice" and "kind" to such children is not likely to be effective in breaking the negative cycle. But a teacher of young children who becomes alert to the possible development of the nega-tive cycle can use a range of strategies with which to break it. Taking action in such cases is one of the very many important roles of teach-ers of young children.

Before leaving this principle of "choice of error," I would like to offer the suggestion that we also take opportunities as they arise to teach young children strategies by which they can let us know that they do not want help at a given moment. In this way they can pro-tect themselves from excessive assistance or solicitude. As appropriate occasions arise, the teacher can suggest to children that when they want to continue to work out problems by themselves they can just say to the adult, "Thanks, but I am OK now!" or "Thanks, I don't need help yet," or something similar that is polite and clear. In this way, the adult gets a signal to back off from being perhaps excessively helpful, and the child can protect him/herself from such excesses.

Teaching at just about every level presents constant moments of decision-making. When making decisions about important aspects of teaching it may help to make explicit to oneself, or in discussions with involved colleagues, what the potential errors associated with each possible course of action might be, and then take time to examine each of the potential errors as thoroughly as possible. It helps to list the possible advantages and disadvantages or errors of each possible course of action before making a final decision. Unfortunately, much of our work with young children involves "on the spot" decisions that don't allow time for thoughtful reflections concerning which might be the "least worst error."

I recall many years ago from somewhere in the upper reaches of the University of Illinois a strong recommendation was made to all professors to use end-of-semester examinations as a basis for grading students, particularly in classes for undergraduates. At that time I had not been using final examinations. No doubt that was partly due to the fact that I very rarely taught undergraduates. When I did take up the recommendation to give final exams I had the impression that students paid attention to lectures, readings, and discussions in terms of what was examinable. Many asked questions like, "Which pages will be covered on the exam?" I frequently answered such questions with the question, "Does this mean that you won't read material that is not going to be included on the exam?" To which the answer was always, "Yes." This answer certainly made sense; it is a good example of adaptive behavior and probably the kind of behavior that helped to make possible these students' admission to the University of Illinois, which was based on their secondary school achievements and SAT scores.

On the other hand, with or without a final exam, I always asked graduate students to "grade" themselves on the same three criteria on which I also would grade them. These criteria were first, the extent to which they believe their own knowledge and understanding of early childhood education had increased and deepened considering the knowledge and understanding of the field they had at the beginning of the semester. The students in my graduate courses were very diverse in background, culture, extent and variety of teaching experience, and level of graduate studies. Therefore, they certainly had not started the semester in my class at the same places of either experience or knowledge and understanding of the field. The second criterion they were to grade themselves on was the extent to which they worried or "agonized" over the issues raised, discussed, and read about in the course. The third criterion was the extent to which they engaged in studying with and learning from other members of the class. Without the exam, it is very likely that few students completed all the recommended reading. But their participation in discussions, the content of their reaction papers (not required) indicating and explicating their reactions to the lectures, discussions and to the readings were typically thoughtful and promising of continued interest in deepening their knowledge and understanding of the field – especially so when no final examination was required.

This experience suggested to me that one of the major advantages of including a final examination was that students were more likely to undertake the recommended reading; but, on the other hand, my hypothesis was that one of the disadvantages or "errors" of using formal examinations is that students' dispositions to engage in their own analysis and reflection on the issues would not be awakened and strengthened. It would be interesting to be able to test the hypothesis and establish empirically which was the "least worst" error: *to include* versus *to omit* final examinations in graduate courses. Perhaps the best "error" depends on specific characteristics of the individual students. But I think a main lesson here is that it is unlikely that choices among alternative courses of action on important matters can ever be error free. I selected the error that I believed had a greater chance of strengthening in students a disposition to engage in life-long learning. But that remains an untested hypothesis.

Principle No. 3. All Relationships Must Have Content

At about the age of nineteen, while Steve was an undergraduate student at the University of Illinois, and living with a friend in a nearby neighborhood, he frequently came home on weekends to visit and to do his laundry. Depending on the season, we often took a walk together on these afternoons. On one such occasion he and

I enjoyed a leisurely walk together on a Saturday afternoon as he waited for his laundry to dry. As usual, our conversations gave us a chance to catch up on our respective activities and ideas, and particularly for me to learn about his reactions to the various courses and musical activities in which he was participating.

I cannot recall how it came up, but it seemed to be a rather sudden change of topic during one of these talks when Steve put to me the question, "How do you decide whom to marry?" That was the classic *intellectual emergency* created by what seemed at first to be a casual question from Steve. He did not indicate that he was seriously considering marriage at the time, though my vague recollection is that he was enjoying the company of a flautist in the orchestra in which he was participating.

I must admit that my first impulse was to answer this difficult question by saying something like, "In your case, it had better be somebody wealthy!" At that time, I had very much in mind the average cost of a decent cello, among other things. But, his question was a serious one, and I resisted the temptation to share my first reaction. I cannot recall having given this topic any real thought before that particular moment, though I probably had done so myself as a teenager. Once again, Steve put me into an emergency situation in which I had to make up something in a hurry!

My reaction to this tricky question was also tempered by the fact that he was the first of our three children to fall in love at about the age of sixteen. We all struggled with that experience in many ways. But since that early experience he had reported on several other absorbing amours. So I had to come up with something fairly quickly, as usual. My somewhat delayed response was, "I think you have to decide whether or not the two of you can go on growing in each other's company." I went on to suggest to Steve that when we first fall in love, the content of the relationship is largely about the relationship itself, and how we can't go on living except when we are together, and so forth. The underlying principle that I suggested was that all relationships have to have content for a good marriage to grow. People cannot have relationships – good ones or bad ones – in a vacuum. There has to be content that matters to the members of the relationship. The content has to be significant or important to the participants. It does not necessarily have to be pleasant or fun – but it does have to matter, at least most of the time. By the way, Steve didn't marry until 20 years later!

The idea that relationships have to have content led me soon thereafter to thinking about the content of the relationships between teachers and children especially in early childhood education settings. Whenever I had the opportunity to spend time in preschool and kindergarten classes I tried to ascertain what constituted the main content of interactions between the children and their teachers and the children with each other. The more chances I had to observe life in classroom settings – around the US and other countries - the more I became aware of how little intellectual content there was in these interactions, and how much of it was dominated by routines and rules of the daily schedule of events. By intellectual content I mean children's questions, ideas, theories, hypotheses, thoughts about their plans, and so forth.

Awareness of the content of interactions in preschool settings led me to thinking further about a fairly widespread tendency among those who make many policy and administrative decisions about early education. Political and other public commentators on the education of young children seem to think that we are faced with a choice between just two alternatives if not opposite curriculum approaches: a fairly traditional approach consisting largely of play, coloring within the lines, and cutting and pasting as well as story time, etc., versus a curriculum approach dominated by academic formal instruction lessons. Such oversimplified contrasts in curriculum approaches probably apply to some aspects of primary education as well.

A major issue in conceptualizing our choices this way - as though these were the only two options - is that while aspects of both of them have a place in preschool education, they both neglect the importance of children's intellectual development during these early years. Many basic intellectual dispositions are probably inborn – granted that they may be stronger in some of us than in others. It seems reasonable to assume that for example, all of us are born with the disposition to make the best sense we can of our experiences, to be nosey, to try to find out things, to analyze cause-effect relationships in the events and other phenomena around us, and so forth. When the development of the intellect is addressed in an early childhood curriculum then the content of interaction between teachers and children as well as the children with each other would include many genuine opportunities to try to explain things, to analyze, hypothesize, to make predictions, to persist in solving problems, and apply fairly frequently these important intellectual dispositions. Opportunities to actually engage in these basic intellectual dispositions can contribute to strengthening children's in-born dispositions to make the best sense they can of their experiences and their environments.

One of the many reasons why I have given much time and effort over many years helping teachers to incorporate the Project Approach (Katz & Chard, 2000; Helm & Katz, 2001) into the early years curriculum is because it involves children in investigations of their environments and experiences worth understanding more accurately and more deeply. Projects are investigations about how things work, where things come from, what they are made of, who does what in our environment, what tools they use, and so forth, providing genuine opportunities for children to enact their inborn intellectual dispositions to learn.

Recent research in the UK has highlighted the long term benefits of what is referred to as "sustained shared thinking." in which the adults interact with children in ways that sustain their thinking about a particular topic and/or activity in the classroom in a wide variety of ways (Sylva et. al, 2004; Dowling, 2005). In order for such sustained interaction to occur there must be content of significance to the participants; it doesn't have to be fun or exciting, but it does have to be interesting or to matter to the participants.

While spontaneous play is clearly valuable to all aspects of children's growth, development and learning (Pramling Samuelsson & Fleer, in press), extended in-depth investigations of elements of their environments worth understanding more deeply can be expected to enrich children's thinking and strengthen and support their intellectual dispositions. As already suggested, the critics of the "play and paste" curriculum tend to believe that formal academic instruction in early literacy and numeracy skills in order to achieve "school readiness" offers the only other option to a play-based approach. I suggest, however, that excessive emphasis during the preschool period on such de-contextualized formal lessons may undermine children's inborn intellectual dispositions. Some children may even come to think of their own questions and hunches as wrong or dumb, and give up trying to make sense of their experiences.

The content of interaction in the traditional and conventional "free play/cut-and-paste" preschool and kindergarten program typically focuses on the classroom routines: "It's time to put things away," "It's time to clean up." In such programs the content of interaction is about when and where to stand in line, calls to group time, reminders of the rules and routines, and other "housekeeping" processes that occur when the teachers are not reading stories or engaging children in musical or physical activities. These experiences are not harmful to children. However, the question that has occurred to me very often is whether there is sufficient frequency of mind-engaging content to support the development of children's intellectual dispositions during a period of rapid growth. Again, while daily but brief exercises in phonics, phonemes and rhymes led by the teacher are not necessarily harmful to young children, they may have long-term, mind-deadening effects on them if they are offered too frequently or are too dominant in the curriculum, (Stipek, 2005).

The emphasis on testing, benchmarks and standards since the introduction of the No Child Left Behind legislation seems to contribute to increased emphasis on formal academic instruction. The goal of narrowing the gap between the school readiness of children from low- and high-income families seems to provoke insistence on more formal instruction for the low-income children and to ignore their intellectual capabilities. I suggest that just because young children have not been read to, or been urged to read simple signs, or to start writing their names, and in other ways to be informally introduced to elements of literacy and numeracy, does not mean that they lack intellectual dispositions such as those suggested above. In addition, it seems useful to keep in mind that daily life in complex poor neighborhoods may provoke many kinds of intellectual processes (i.e., attempts to make sense of the complex environment and how to predict what might happen, when and where).

Furthermore, it seems more appropriate to me to help young children begin to use basic literacy and measurement facts and skills in the service of their intellectual endeavors. Teachers have so often told me stories about very young children who, when engaged in investigations in projects, have asked for help with how to write the caption of a drawing they have completed, or how to measure various attributes and aspects of the things they are investigating.

A related issue is the recent research indicating that from the very beginning of life, development of a variety of basic cognitive capabilities benefit greatly from what we might call continuous contingent interaction. One of the best examples of such continuous contingent interactions is conversation, namely a sequence of contingent responses of one person to another even though the response of one might just be a nod, a frown, or a laugh. Early and frequent opportunities to participate in such extended interactions are believed to help build the neurological connections between the mid-brain area where emotions and motives are experienced, and the prefrontal cortex where planning, effort and self-regulation processes occur (Blair, 2002; Rothbart & Posner, 2005). However, if there is to be extended interaction in the form of conversations, there must be something to converse about: something that matters to the conversationalists. As I suggested earlier, the content does not have to be fun or amusing, or even necessarily interesting; but it does have to be meaningful and significant to the participants. The availability of significant content is another reason why good project work in the form of investigations carried out by the children should be a regular part of the curriculum starting in the early years of preschool education.

I am often taken aback by the ways I have observed many teachers talk to young children. It is clear that teachers and most others want to be kind and accepting of the young children. Perhaps the constant use of sweet tones and unreal phrases may just be an occupational hazard of working with young children over a period of long time. We also have come to offer children very frequent praise as in, "Good job!" or "Fantastic!" and other catch phrases. Sometimes I think that we have simply over-corrected for the practices when I was a child many years ago and adults withheld compliments or praise for fear that children would become conceited.

But children are not likely to be hurt when we speak to them directly and clearly and calmly instead of super-sweetly. I once observed a young enthusiastic and dedicated kindergarten teacher who had put on the top right-hand corner of her large blackboard a very colorful smiling tiger made of cardboard about three feet long and two feet tall. I can't recall now what its name was. But every time the children became a bit rowdy the teacher raised her voice and said, "The tiger (by its pet name) is upset that you are so noisy!" The children seemed to understand the game she was playing. But why an adult would ask children to respond to the feelings of a cardboard tiger and not to the judgment of their teacher is something of a mystery to me. Why would a teacher say to a child who just grabbed a stapler from another one, "We don't do that in this class!" when the child just did it? Practices like these create a phony classroom culture that fails to involve children in making good sense of their experience and environment.

Sometimes I hear teachers refer to themselves by their own name, as for example Mrs. Jones saying to the children, "Mrs. Jones is waiting for you to sit down!" Perhaps this kind of phoniness is a long established part of the elementary education culture. I am reminded here of reading some time ago of a study showing that teachers tend to teach the way they remember being taught in first grade – even though they are now teaching three- and four-year olds. Perhaps it is in this way that long-term traditions – welcome as well as unwelcome ones – seem to persist and to be re-enacted year after year.

Another pattern of interaction often observed is that of teachers saying to children things like: "You need to turn around!" and "You need to sit still!" But these are very unlikely to be the children's "needs." It would be more genuine for the teacher to say, in a clear and matter-of-fact tone "I want you to turn around!" or "I want you to sit still!" And then change the subject – change the content of the interaction. Once again, the issue of the content of relationships arises. It is relatively easy to change the subject or content of interaction when there are many interesting things in progress, such as extended investigations of things worth learning more about. But if the curriculum offers little for involving children in genuine activities, changing the content of interaction might be more difficult.

I suggest then that it is a good idea for young children – and perhaps older ones too - to get clear messages from real and genuine persons. This implies that all of us must strive to resist the temptation to be phony with children. My hunch is that in their relationships with both parents and teachers, children accept and maybe even welcome genuine and clear messages about what is expected from the important adults in their lives and about what these adults believe is right and valued. So, as I have already suggested, is seems best to say clearly what behavior is wanted, and then, once stated - change the content of the interaction to something that matters in terms of learning and getting on with meaningful tasks, and the like.

Principle No. 4 Offer Learners Informative Feedback

As part of his undergraduate study of music Steve was able to take piano lessons. On one of his weekend visits home during that period, I asked him how the piano lessons were going. Steve's unexpected response was, "O.K. But my teacher! Being her student is like sucking on a bland lollipop. She doesn't realize that her smiles are no substitute for information!" How was I to respond to that one? As we talked more about this very pleasant teacher and Steve's desire for more specifics and clearer guidance I had been following the progress of a fairly substantial body of research concerning the differential effects of various kinds of feedback (see Chapter 2, Katz & Chard, 2000).

The essence of the research on these matters suggests that general positive feedback to young children may keep them producing work and activities of various kinds for a while, but it is unlikely to encourage real interest, absorption and involvement in the work at hand (Lepper, Iyengar & Corpus, 2005). For the latter, what is required is informative feedback, not necessarily either positive or negative in nature, but task-specific and meaningful and offered in a matter-of-fact tone (See also Flum and Kaplan, 2006).

The excessive use by teachers of expressions such as "Good job!" and "Well done!" may interfere with strengthening the important disposition called *interest* and other aspects of intrinsic motivation. The term interest is not easy to define. I find it helpful to define it as the disposition to lose oneself in something outside of one-self – a topic or a task or a hobby. There has been some indication in research that early in the elementary school years children come to believe that achievements or activities for which teachers give them rewards are those that no-one in his or her right mind would like doing or want to do voluntarily! (See also Flum & Kaplan, (2006).

In connection with this aspect of evaluating children's work and progress, I have frequently recommended to teachers to take opportunities from time to time to encourage children to evaluate their own progress, especially as they grow older. But even the young children can occasionally and informally be encouraged to inspect their own efforts - not in terms of whether their accomplishments are good or bad or right or wrong, but according to other criteria against which to assess their progress. For example, depending some-what on the tasks at hand and on the ages of the children, a teacher could encourage children to evaluate whether they consider their work (e.g. a model, construction, or drawing, etc.) to be as complete as they would like it to be, or whether there are sufficient details in the work, or whether they have included clear examples of the points being made, and so forth. All of these kinds of examinations of their own work are easily and realistically incorporated into project work, even with young children.

As children enter the kindergarten and primary grades, for example, teachers can take opportunities periodically to meet with the children in the class individually and to summarize with them the main topics and skills the class has been working on. After intro-ducing the subject of the recent work of the class, the teacher can then ask the child something like, "Of all the things we have been working on, what are the ones you feel you are doing well? The next question might be, "What aspects of our work do you think you need to work harder on?" This can be followed with a final question that might be something like, "What aspects of our work do you think you need someone to help you with?" In any class there might be one or two children who claim to be brilliant in everything. There might also be a few who might make the opposite self-assessment and claim to need help with everything and maybe they do. However, the chances are that by the early elementary grades most children will be fairly realistic about their own progress, especially if the teacher has developed a class culture of serious examination of how various aspects of their work are progressing.

Young children who are just learning to write can begin to acquire the habit of doing first and second, and even third drafts. I have more than one hundred papers in print and still even today depend greatly on colleagues' willingness to read first, second and third drafts. I cannot imagine proceeding without the helpful feedback of others.

I am not aware of any research evidence on the effects such a strategy of children's self-evaluations might have, though I have tried for several years to persuade graduate students to obtain some.

Principle No. 5. Offer ideas a child can put in his/her psychological pocket

Following two good years of experience in a cooperative nursery school, Steve entered kindergarten. The teacher was the same one his brother had, and I had every reason to expect that things would go well. About three weeks after school began, Steve said to me on the way home from school, "When we have group time, I feel cold inside." I believed then and still do today, that I knew what he meant. It is not an easy feeling to describe, but perhaps we could say it is a kind of loneliness or longing to belong, or something like feeling cut off from warm connections with important others.

What would be a helpful way to respond to such a maternal "emergency"? I didn't say to Steve what my mother would surely have said to me – something like, "What's the matter with you? All the other children are having a good time!" I simply asked him calmly, "What time do you have group time?" He said he didn't know. He hadn't yet learned to read the clock and I was not aware of the time schedule in kindergarten. I then asked him to tell me what was the usual morning sequence of events. When he finished describing their usual morning routines I told him that I thought they probably had group time around 10.30 AM. I then said to him something like, "Tomorrow when you are in group time, you look up at the clock on the wall behind the teacher. I will look at the clock at that time too, and remember that I'll be thinking of you and then you will feel better."

I had long forgotten this whole matter when in 1983 I served as a Fulbright Professor at the University of Baroda in India for three months. During that time, Steve wrote me only one letter – one which he neglected to post, by the way, and that he gave to me when I returned to Illinois! But, as you can see in the copy of it (See Part VI, page 73), he said, "I feel you so close to me. When I think of you, you are here with me, just like when I needed you at school way back."

I have often referred to this kind of strategy as putting something in the child's psychological pocket to take with him or her to use as a source of comfort and reassurance. I did not offer a rabbit's foot or a good luck charm, a superstition or any other kind of falsehood. Over the years others have told me of other apparently effective examples of how to put something into a child's psychological pocket. Among many examples parents have shared with me, I have always appreciated one given to me by a mother of a young boy. She said that he had some separation difficulties when he started school, and she would kiss her child's right hand fist before leaving him and suggest to him that if he became lonely or wished his mother was with him, he could rub the hand on his cheek and be reminded of those by whom he is deeply love, and then he would feel better. The mother did not try to talk him out of it or to deny his feelings. What she did was express understanding with honesty and simplicity, and she reported that it took him no more than about a week to adapt to the new situation competently.

During his early elementary school years, Steve came home complaining about a teacher who, he said, wanted everybody in the class to make the same picture; but, as usual, he wanted to make a different one, a unique one. He seemed to be saying that he was afraid he would lose his own ideas if he made the same picture as all his classmates. At the moment of complaint I was preoccupied with other matters and was not prepared for an extended discussion of the issues involved. I recall having said something like, "Don't worry. You will always have your own ideas. It won't be spoiled by doing what this teacher wants you to do." On further reflection a bit later, when I had more time, I thought again about the important part my role was to help my children to cope with the situations they encountered. We don't have to agree with our children that every frustrating or difficult situation is a tragedy. But it seems to me that an important role for adults is helping children to cope with daily ups and downs, and not to deny them or even try to solve them for the child.

Another way of thinking along similar lines about our responsibilities as adults is to help children gradually learn to distinguish between what really is a tragedy and what is not. It is, of course, appropriate to feel sorrow and sadness for the loss of, or separation from, a loved one and other serious problems. But incidents like failing to get a turn to play with a favorite toy are not tragedies. It would not be a good idea for a teacher or parent to scorn the child's excessive emotional reaction. But the adult can say to a child, in a tone reflecting understanding, something like, "I know you are disappointed that you didn't get a turn. But there's tomorrow to look forward to," or something like, "Some days are tough, but I think you'll make it okay." Then change the content of the interaction to something real and relevant to the situation and forthcoming activities.

The underlying principle here is to offer children reasonable and understandable coping strategies. We cannot always change the environment to suit our own children, though we might wish to.

A main focus of our roles as parents is not only to ensure that our children are kept out of danger, but also to help them to cope competently with the actual situations they encounter. At the same time we can also work on changing undesirable or dangerous situations as appropriate. But it is very unlikely that any given context, such as a school, will be equally accommodating for every single child on every single day.

Along similar lines, I suggest that one of the main goals of parents and teachers of young children is not so much to get them to achieve independence, but to help them to develop what we could call *competent interdependence*. All of us depend more or less on many others near (and not so near) to us. Learning to cope competently with those upon whom we depend in so many ways takes time and certainly seems to require experience with helpful and understanding adults.

School environments can be only just so flexible; they are, after all, institutions governed by rules and regulations believed to serve the best interests of all concerned. It is, for example, unlikely that any individual child will like or be equally comfortable with every teacher she or he will have. The parents' role in the less desirable cases of teacher-child relationships is to help the child to cope with it rather than to try to change the whole school. We can remind parents that, "After all, your child still has you!"

Principle No. 6 The Soundness of an Idea Is Not Related to the Number of People Who Subscribe to It

On one occasion when Steve was almost at the end of his high school years I was busy getting ready to leave for a speaking engagement across the country, as was often the case. Steve asked me where I was going and what I would be doing when I got there. When I explained that I would be giving a talk at a conference of teachers he asked me, "Doesn't it make you feel good that other people want to listen to you?" This query was not one of the typical intellectual emergencies with Steve that I had become used to. But it seemed to be an interesting provocation to consider the ramifications of his question. My response to him was the question, "But, Steve, what if I'm wrong?" He seemed surprised by my question, and he didn't have an answer to it. So I continued by suggesting, as a principle, that the soundness of an idea is not related to the number of people who subscribe to it.

This observation or principle, as I have come to think of it since then, was not totally out of line with previous conversations we had had around the dinner table in connection with the rapidly developing Watergate crisis and the grave accusations being broadcast about the behavior of then President Richard Nixon; the fact that millions of people had voted for him did not make his positions necessarily right, or for that matter, wrong either. Numbers of voters tells us who agrees or disagrees with whom, but not necessarily who is right.

I indicated to Steve that when a great idea is developed, it doesn't become greater once everyone knows about it or accepts it. Galileo got into lots of trouble by suggesting that the earth was not the center of the universe. His ideas were not more true when finally the rest of the world agreed with him. The Hungarian obstetrician, Ignaz Semmelweiss, was working as an intern in Vienna in 1847, when he made the shocking discovery that puerperal fever (child bed fever) was transmitted from one patient to another in maternity wards by physicians who did not wash their hands after performing autopsies. When he proposed hand-washing as a potentially life-saving practice, he was dismissed from his profession and eventually ended up in an insane asylum. However, he was right! I pointed out also to Steve that when Newton formulated the concept of gravity or Einstein developed the concept of relativity, these concepts were just as true or valid when they were the only individuals who knew them as when the rest of the world became informed of them and subsequently accepted them. In other words, when it comes to ideas, we are essentially on our own. Our best recourse is to set out our ideas as clearly as we can where others can examine them, agree and disagree with them, test them, and accept or reject them. But that is one of the reasons why interaction with others whose experiences and views are different from our own is so important and useful. It is another reason why we have to try to keep abreast of relevant research. But, essentially, when it comes to the development and presentation of ideas, we're on our own.

Principle No. 7 Teach Children to Use Their Own Experience as Data

When Steve was in the first grade he had to undergo a series of dental treatments to deal with various irregularities, one of which was an extra tooth. This meant that I had to pick him up at school several times over a period of several weeks to take him to the dentist. On most such occasions it seemed to take forever to get him ready to leave his classroom and the school. He couldn't find his lunch box, or misplaced his jacket, or had some other excuse why he wasn't ready to leave the school, even though I repeatedly reminded him that we would be late if he didn't hurry up.

After several such incidents when he seemed to be dragging his feet I realized that he was clearly reluctant to return to the dentist's chair. Who could blame him for that? I would certainly wonder about a six-year-old who would be enthusiastic about such a rendezvous. But in this kind of emergency, I felt that I had to make up something in a hurry. I then asked Steve if he remembered what it was like the last time he had been to the dentist. He replied with a rather grim expression that he did. I asked him then if he remembered how uncomfortable he was in the dentist's chair, to which he said, again grimly, "Yes." I then asked him if he remembered how annoying it was to have all that stuff the dentist put in his mouth, and again he replied bleakly, "Yes." I then asked him if he remembered how relieved he was when it was all over, and he responded cheerfully, "Oh, yeah!" which I followed by saying "It's going to be just like that again." He then seemed to straighten up and approach the car for the ride to the dentist with greater ease.

Steve says now that he vividly recalls sitting in the dentist's chair and as Dr. Appleton entered the room and said, "So, Steve, how are we today?" he replied, "Actually, I'm really glad to be here!" I could never have imagined that kind of a response from the reluctant youngster a few weeks earlier!

The underlying principle here is to take occasions as they arise to help children to use their own experience as data upon which they can derive a strategy for coping with similar ones.

Often parents tell their young ones just before they start kindergarten that they will make lots of friends, do lots of fun things and have a good time. Perhaps so. But it might be wise to add to these promises something like, "But there will be moments when you wish you were at home. But those moments will pass." In this way, if such moments do arise, the child has been forewarned, knows that low moments will pass, and therefore is less likely to become unstrung by the feelings of distress that arise.

Principle No. 8. Parenting and Teaching Often Require Feed-Forward Justification

When Steve was about ten or eleven years old and his Dad brought him home from his regular Saturday cello lesson, he came directly to me in the kitchen where I was preparing lunch, and he said, "Now Mom, no matter what I tell you, make me practice! Even if I say I already know the piece, even if I say my fingers are sore, or I have a stomach ache" and he continued with his list of other common excuses. I assured him that I would "make him practice" no matter what excuses were offered. I wasn't keen on this part of my parenting role. But I stuck to my end of the bargain as well as I could for many years

About three or four years later Steve and his Dad were practicing a Vivaldi sonata in preparation for a forthcoming recital. In the middle of the first movement Steve stopped playing and called out to me to the kitchen and urged me to come and listen to them. With great pleasure, I did so. As they progressed through the first movement Steve suddenly stopped playing, turned to me and said, "Mom, if you hadn't nagged me I wouldn't be able to make this wonderful sound!" I wasn't thrilled with the characterization as a nagger; however, there was a hint of gratitude in the declaration.

Along similar lines Steve recalls at about the age of 12 putting down his cello and walking into the kitchen to make the following announcement, "Mom, I've decided to quit playing the cello." My response to this shocker was, "I see. Well, why don't you think a little longer before making your decision final." Steve recalls returning to the living room where he had been practicing to "think a little longer" and thinking, "Okay, I could quit now and never pick up the cello again. But later on I might wish I had kept playing. If I don't keep playing, I won't know what I was missing. And something tells me the cello could be a very important part of my future. I'd better keep practicing. And so I did."

The essence of these incidents reminded me of the concept of the "feed forward" problem that I had first heard discussed by my late esteemed colleague at the University of Illinois, Professor Harry Broudy who talked and wrote about *much education*. He suggested that *much education* consists of giving learners information and knowledge they do not yet want or experiences they cannot at the time imagine ever needing. In a deep sense what Steve was saying to me way back around the age of ten was something like, "Make me do what I don't like doing now, but later on when I look back on this not very pleasant experience, I will be glad or even grateful, that you did so." In other words, the essence of the problem is that, as children get older, parents and teachers are often in situations in which they must insist on children undergoing experiences of little immediate interest, current or apparent value, but that can be expected to reap benefits later on.

My own parents used to say things like, "Some day you'll thank me for this!" when insisting on undertaking an unpleasant task. The adult in situations like these must be clear in his or her own thinking of how to weigh the benefits of short-term unhappiness with long-term satisfaction and fulfillment.

The concept of the "feed forward" problem then became an organizing issue in research on teacher education (see Katz & Raths, 1992) When it comes to pre-service teacher education, the "feed forward" problem, according to Broudy, consists of providing students with answers to questions they have not yet asked and with strategies and solutions for problems not yet encountered. In addition, it suggests that when their questions are asked and answered, candidates may feel satisfied at the time, but when they evaluate their pre-service education retrospectively – perhaps one or two years later when on the job – their evaluations may become more negative. Similarly, pre-service experiences evaluated negatively at the time they are experienced may, in retrospect, be re-evaluated positively once on the job. In other words, they would be saying what Steve predicted he would say – something like, "I didn't want to do X then, but now I am glad I did it because I wouldn't be able to do so well what I can do now without that previous experience."

Thus, teacher educators must determine the appropriateness of what they offer to students on bases other than their appreciation or enjoyment at the time. Empirical research that would help us to make such determinations is not, unfortunately, available and not easy to conduct.

Along similar lines, it was at about this same time that Steve and I started to collect paradoxes. This was provoked by Steve's observation upon returning from one of his cello lessons during his university training when he said, "The more I learn about how to play the cello, the more difficult it is to play well." I suggested that this observation fit the definition of a paradox, namely a statement that seems self-contradictory. I suggested that what was happening was that his criteria for good performance were growing, deepening and becoming much more detailed.

Another paradox that I recall, though I am not sure whether I shared it with him, was that having much musical talent may not lead to more accomplished performances than those of performers of less talent. The reasoning here is that in the latter cases the learners are more likely to develop a strong disposition to work hard and, therefore, ultimately to become more accomplished than perhaps a more talented student to whom much skill was easily achieved. Much of what was involved in learning to play the cello came easily to Steve. But, perhaps partly my fault, he never really learned to work hard or to practice the long hours that top performance levels require. Another similar paradox we discussed and that most of us become aware of sooner or later was that the more we know, the more aware we become of how much more there is to know. I cannot now recall the other paradoxes in our collection; but I do recall that gathering them served as the basis for many delightful discussions with him. Suffice it to say that life in general, and teaching in particular, is full of paradoxes and troubling dilemmas as well (see Katz & Raths, 1992).

Principle No. 9. Teaching is often about helping the learners to understand better and/or differently something they already know

As Steve made his way through the early years of school he presented a number of challenges (as well as many joys) to his parents and teachers. On one occasion I recall early in his first grade year trying to help him with some fairly simple arithmetic processes. He was attempting to complete an exercise, the details of which I can no longer recall. It had something to do with classifying items in groups of ones, twos and threes. When we finished the discussion he said to me, "I already knew that because I sometimes go up the stairs, one- at-a-time, two-at-a-time, or three-at-a-time and I take less steps when I go two-at-a-time than when I go one-at-a-time."

This incident and several similar later ones caused me to think that one role of a teacher is to help the learners to understand what they already know and about experiences they have already had, *differently*. Ideally, the different or new ways of thinking about the phenomena in question are more accurate and more useful than were the previous ways.

In other words, teaching is not only about **_in_**struction of new knowledge, or explanations of complex phenomena, but is often about re-**_con_**struction of how the learner already understands a particular phenomenon the teacher wants him or her to master. One such example comes to mind of when I was conducting a workshop with a large group of Head Start teachers on the teacher's role in the development of social competence in the early years. When I solicited questions, one teacher who already had some twenty-five years of experience working in Head Start shared her frustrations concerning a particular boy. She explained that every morning he got to class a bit late and went directly to where classmates were building with blocks and knocked down their structures. I asked her gently, "Where are you when this happens?" She replied that she was at the door greeting children and their parents or grandparents upon their arrival. I then asked her, "What have you tried so far?" She then reported that every morning she sits down with him and explains to him that the children whose constructions he damaged "don't like it when you do that!" My (gentle) response was, "He already knows that." The teacher was taken aback by this comment as she realized that for some weeks she was spending some fifteen minutes every morning preaching to the child something he clearly already understood. This boy had her scheduled to give him intense company every morning. It is difficult to be sure of his motives – perhaps he just liked sitting with her and having her full attention daily. Apparently he also showed off this one-on-one situation to the other children as they passed by. The point here is that teacher now understood her pattern of response to this repeated behavior *differently* from previously. We then discussed matters: first, of being near him to prevent the behavior pattern; second, to develop a relationship with him that would have different and more interesting content; and third, she learned about the importance of stating clearly to a child what behavior you do not want, and what behavior you do want. This kind of pattern of disruptive behavior reminds us that the ability to change the content of a relationship is to a large extent dependent upon the richness of the curriculum.

An important question in such cases is: Does the curriculum offer content that matters to the children? Does the curriculum include ideas and activities worthy of young children's interests? As I have already suggested, engaging your children in in-depth investigations of interesting events and phenomena around them that provides rich content for interaction is one of the many reasons why the Project Approach is recommended (Katz & Chard, 2000).

I have repeatedly heard from teachers who implement the project approach that the frequency of disruptive behavior was greatly reduced as the children took over their investigating and associated responsibilities. There is, unfortunately, good reason to believe that when the curriculum is uninteresting, even boring in some cases, children will make the environment lively and interesting in their own ways. This might be especially the case for children growing in cultures and environments in which they are expected to be assertive and active, rather than passive and demur. In good project work, children are actively engaged in investigating things around them, representing their findings in various media and sharing their findings with each other, and thus are involved in active and assertive rather than passive and reactive roles.[1]

Principle No. 10. Teach Children to Take Pleasure in Each Other's Gifts

Our youngest child, Miriam, began piano and violin lessons around the age of eight, and made fairly normal though not spectacular progress for a few years. At about the age of fourteen she decided she wanted to study voice. She soon started with a voice teacher and seemed to have found her favorite musical instrument. At about that time I was making frequent trips to Washington, DC, working with the National Head Start Bureau on the Planned Variation Experiment and several related projects designed to resolve countless issues concerning the Head Start curriculum.

On one such occasion, I arrived in Washington and made my usual phone call to home to let my husband know how and when I could be reached and to catch up on various other details involved in the lives of the three teenagers. When Steve answered the phone I asked, "What's new?" and when he said, "Nothing," I made my habitual response with, "What kind of nothing?" and so the conversation went, as usual. My husband was not at home; he was out playing tennis. So I asked Steve to take down my phone numbers and to be sure to give them to his Dad and to ask him to call me on his return home. "Okay, Mom," said Steve, and I said "Fine, I'll see you when I get home on Thursday, okay? Bye." Then he quickly

---

1   For more information about the Project Approach and examples of projects see <illinoisPIP.org>. Also, each issue of the journal *Early Childhood Research and Practice* has a project included in it www.ecrp.uiuc.edu in both English and Spanish and can be downloaded without cost.

said, "Wait a minute, Mom. There's something I have to tell you!" My heart began to sink at the thought he had some unwelcome news to share with me. After all, he was just sixteen-years-old! "Alright," I said, crossing my fingers that there would be no crises looming ahead for the family. At that point he said to me in his usual thoughtful way, "It is such a joy watching Miriam discover her voice." We then chatted briefly about what he had heard as she practiced for her voice lessons, and I agreed, of course, that this was a source of pleasure for us all.

How different, I thought, was this response to a sibling's gifts from those with which I grew up. I am one of three daughters – no brothers. I have a twin sister (See Part VI), ten minutes younger than I, and we had a sister seven years older than we were. Both my siblings were artists, and clearly so from early childhood. Both also played the piano and could sing well. I struggled, willingly but not very effectively, with trying to master the violin. My mother (who had perfect pitch and was an accomplished violinist) told me that when it came to joining in the singing, I had a nice enough voice, but that it was usually in the wrong key, so I should be quiet. Unfortunately, she was right about that!

When my twin sister won the scholarship to the Hammersmith School of Art (in London) at the age of twelve, the same scholarship our eldest sister had won at that age, my father complained to me that perhaps if I hadn't been such a day-dreamer, I could have got one too. What he should have said was something like, "Isn't it wonderful that another one of us has this great opportunity?" and thereby encouraged me to take pleasure from my sisters' gifts and to feel included in the celebration.

Steve's reaction to his sister's growing vocal abilities reminded me that it is a good idea to actively teach children, within the family (as well as within a class) to take pleasure in each other's gifts and accomplishments. I recall observing a nursery school teacher in the west of England many years ago while she was mounting one of the children's beautiful paintings on the wall. As she was completing the task, two lively four-year-old boys were scurrying past her, and she stopped them and said to them, "Take a look at Jeffrey's painting.

Isn't that wonderful?" she said. She then casually pointed to some of the painting's special features. When she finished her brief talk about the painting, the two boys turned around toward the classroom looking for the painter. When they saw him they shouted across the room, "Jolly good, Jeffrey!" and moved on with their plans.

In no way did the teacher imply something like, "If you worked harder, you could do that too." The teacher implied no element of competition or comparison, and as far as I could tell, nor was there any hint to the passersby that they should do better or try harder. It is often said in families, "When your brother was your age he could already do X or Y," and other comments intended to spark competition and catch up behavior.

Encouraging children to enjoy each other's special qualities and their contributions to the accomplishments of the group can enrich the lives of all of them. In the incident described above, the teacher's manner was serious, calm and pleasant; she did not hand out gold stars and pictures of smiling bears with the message "You are special!" The two boys she talked to not only took pleasure in another's accomplishment, but most likely also learned something about what makes a painting interesting and enjoyable to use in their own future work.

Principle No.11. All We Have Is Our Very Best Judgment at the Time

One Friday evening when Steve was about fifteen or sixteen years old he was getting ready to go out for the evening with a school mate I was not very enthusiastic about. I cannot recall the reasons behind my reservations about his companion. My husband was out of town at the time, and I was just apprehensive about our children wandering around on weekend evenings in places I did not know anything about. So, when he was just about to leave the house I said to him, "I want you to be home by ten o'clock!" He responded to my demand with a graceful question, "And what are your reasons for that, Mom?" Thus another classic *intellectual emergency* arose and I had to make up something in a hurry!

I put it to Steve that my insistence on the ten o'clock hour (which I thought of as very liberal) "is my best judgment at the present time." I then elaborated on the "best judgment" notion by pointing out that when his father, a civil engineer, needed to determine the requirements for the safety of a structure he was designing, he was able to refer to the state's structural requirements code books, if necessary. The state codes outlined the state minimal requirements based on extensive study of the strength of materials and the nature of the ground, and so on. But I pointed out to Steve that as his mother I had no code book to refer to. Nobody had been his mother before, and there were no accumulated data to turn to, and I said that, "All I have is my very best judgment." I indicated to him that I thought hard about the bases of the judgments I made, and that it could be that in fifty years' time my judgment will be considered some kind of child abuse; but I could not foretell that possible shift in judgment. He seemed to accept my explanation without difficulty and off he went. I can't recall whether or not he complied with my judgment. But I do recall the feeling that his right to "bitch" about his mother and her rules to his friends was protected, at least!

When it comes to setting restrictions on children, whether as a parent or a teacher there are numerous sources of doubt, especially if the children themselves challenge us. But there is reason to believe that children who are trying to grow in environments without clear boundaries find it hard to organize themselves and to develop a sense of purposefulness and direction.

During the mid-1960's, when I was a graduate student at Stanford University, some of us studied the problems in the surrounding areas encountered by young children of what we came to refer to as "hippie" parents. Many of these parents seemed to us to be very permissive and seemed to urge each other and their children "to let everything hang out," as they used to put it (See Baumrind, 1971). The lack of clear limits or restrictions is likely to leave a child without experience of learning how to identify limits or restrictions, navigate them, and cope with them – all of which are important aspects of learning to adapt to the complex world in which the child will live for the rest of his or her life. Of course, excessive restrictions are also likely to be damaging – thus the principle of optimal effects, i.e., whatever is good for children (or adults) is only good in the right proportions, e.g. attention, affection, food, and so forth. Furthermore, what might be the optimal proportion for one child might not be for another; thus, the importance of observing and knowing each child as well as possible.

In both parenting and teaching, there are multiple situations in which we must make decisions without recourse to relevant and reliable evidence. We are constantly making decisions that require us to exercise our best judgment. On the very numerous occasions when I have spoken to groups of early childhood educators and parents, I have often encouraged them to use opportunities when we come together to share our best judgments, to examine them in the light of whatever research is available, and this way develop and strengthen the disposition to constantly improve those judgments. But again, it seems to me, that one's best judgment is all there is in the many *emergencies* that our children and pupils present to us!

Principle No. 12 Make your mistakes with confidence

Some time around the age of twelve, Steve was practicing the cello with his father at the piano, in preparation for the annual pupil recital organized by his cello teacher. As the time for the recital drew closer Steve shared with me his anxiety about the event. "What if I make a mistake?" he asked. I suggested that making mistakes is always possible and probably the best thing to do is to make your mistakes with confidence! At the time I was probably not very serious about that piece of advice. Nevertheless, the recital was quite successful, and I cannot recall any mistakes. But over the years, I have suggested it as a principle for teachers, too - especially those who are working in new conditions and contexts or attempting to implement new methods and techniques.

The basis for this principle is that it probably is in young children's best interests for the adults responsible for them to approach them with optimal confidence, usually associated with clarity about what is expected and what is valued. However, it is probably a good idea also to make the habit of inspecting one's own behavior on the way home, and asking oneself whether a given strategy was, in retrospect, the most appropriate or effective one, and what might be preferable ways to approach similar situations next time.

Along similar lines, Steve, as a teenager, asked me how I chose my career and how I decided what I wanted to do with my life. He indicated that he didn't know for sure what he wanted to do with his. As I recall, my response was that I thought it best to do whatever is at hand as well and as wholeheartedly as you can, and the rest will follow; and even if it doesn't follow, you will have done what is right. Several years later, when I was nagging him about his plans for his future, he responded by saying that he was doing "what is at hand as well and as wholeheartedly" as he could. Touche!

Conclusion

As I have suggested throughout the discussions of these principles, both parenting and teaching present continuous and numerous predicaments requiring decisions and judgments almost instantly. Invariably, those predicaments described above have led me to reconsider them and to share them with others. Putting them together in this collection is in response to numerous requests to do so. Both Steve and I hope they will be useful and look forward to any comments you wish to share with us.

References

Baumrind, Diana. (1971). Current Patterns of Parental Authority. Developmental Psychology Monographs. 4, 1 – 102.

Blair, C. (2002). School Readiness: Integration of Cognition and Emotion in a Neurobiological Conceptualization of Child Functioning at School Entry. American Psychologist. 57, (2). 111 – 127.

Dowling, Marion. (2005). Supporting Young Children's Sustained Shared Thinking. An Exploration. London, England. UK. British Association for Early Childhood Education. www.early-education.org.uk

Flum, Hanach, & Avi Kaplan. (2006) Exploratory Orientation as an Educational Goal. Educational Psychologist. 41, (2). 99 – 110.

Helm, J. H., & Katz, L. G., (2001). Young Investigators. The Project Approach in the Early Years. New York: Teachers College Press.

Katz, L. G., Chard, S. C. (2000). Second Edition. Engaging Children's Minds. The Project Approach. Stamford, CT. Ablex Publishing Co.

Katz, Lilian G., & Raths, James D. (1992) Six Dilemmas of Teacher Education. Journal of Teacher Education. Vol. 43, No. 5, 376 – 385, Pp.

Lepper, Mark R., Sheena S, Iyengar, Jennifer Hederlong Corpus. (2005). Intrinsic and Extrinsic Motivational Orientations in the Classroom: Age Differences and Academic Correlates. Journal of Educational Psychology. 92, (2) pp. 184 – 196.

Marchand, Gwen & Skinner, Ellen A., (2007) Motivational dynamics of children's academic help-seeking and concealment. Journal of Educational Psychology, 99, (No. 1) pp. 65 – 82

Pramling-Samuelsson, Ingrid & Fleer, Marilyn. Eds. (2009). Play and Learning in Early Childhood settings: International Perspectives. NY. Heinemann

Rothbart, Mary K. & Posner, Michael I. (2005). Genes and Experience in the Development and Executive Attention and Effortful Control. In Jensen, L. A., & Larson, R. W., Eds. (2005). New Horizons in Developmental Theory and Research. San Francisco, CA: Jossey-Bass.

Stipek, Deborah (2005). Early Childhood Education at a Crossroads. Harvard Education Newsletter. Harvard University.

Sylva, K., Melhuuish, E. C., Sammons, P., Siraj-Blatchford, I. & Taggart, B., (2004). The Effective Provision of Pre-school Education (EEPE)

Project: Technical Paper 12 – The Final Report: Effective Pre-school Education. London: DfES/Institute of Education, University of London. www.surestart.gov.uk/schools/ecpe/eppe/inex.htm

Part III. The Last Class Notes[2]

We have lingered over many topics concerning children, parents, teachers and curriculum issues. There is still much to learn about how to help all of our children so that ultimately they can lead good lives. As you return to your work with the children, keep these main points in mind:

#1   Remember that adults know more about almost everything than a small child does -- except what it feels like to be that child, and how the world makes sense to him or her. Those things are the child's expertise which a teacher must learn in order to be able to reach and teach the child.

#2   Remember also that through their behavior children often ask us to help them become the kinds of persons we want them to be, because that is what they want to be. They want to be the kinds of persons we like -- especially while they are still very young! We won't harm them by being clear about what we think is good, right, valuable, and what we believe is worth knowing and understanding.

#3   Take care not to confuse what is exciting, amusing, and fun with what is educative. Excitement is appropriate for entertainment and special occasions; it is short-lived pleasure - easy come, easy go. But what is educative requires sustained effort and involvement, often includes many routine elements, and offers long-term deep satisfaction rather than momentary fun and excitement.

#4   Remember that learning and development take time - change may not! We can change behavior quickly by using threats and punishments; but when these are removed, there is no real development. And remember that it is very hard to grow around impatient people!

#5   Remember also that meaningful relationships have to have content. Relationships cannot be developed in a vacuum; we have

---

2   This is a list of final points I made at the closing of the last class of the semester in graduate classes in which most of the students were teachers of young children. During the nearly forty years of such teaching, the list grew steadily to the length included here. Students often asked for a written version of these notes, but I had neglected to make it available to them.

to relate to each other about something — something that matters to the participants in the relationship. The content of our relationships with children should not be mainly about rules, regulations, and conduct, but about their increasing knowledge and developing understandings of those things within and around them worth knowing more about and understanding more deeply, more fully, and more accurately.

#6   In teaching, as indeed in life, we constantly make decisions. Every decision carries with it its own potential errors. There are probably no error-free decisions. So we have to think ahead about the possible errors embedded in each decision, and then choose the "least worst errors"! In this sense, life is a series of choices of which errors we prefer.

#7   It is a good idea for all of us as teachers to strive for a balance between being sufficiently skeptical to be able to go on learning, and sufficiently convinced about the rightness of what we are doing to be able to go on acting - for to teach is to act. And effective teaching requires optimal confidence in the rightness of our actions.

#8   As teachers, all we have at a given moment--in a given situation--is our own very best judgment. Throughout our professional lives we study and reflect in order to refine that judgment; we exchange with colleagues, consider others' solutions to the problems we face, examine the available evidence - all in order to improve our judgment. But in the last analysis, our very best judgment is all there is.

#9   Teaching involves many conflicting pressures and situations. We cannot respond fully or equally to all of them. We have to decide what is worth making an issue over. Don't make an issue over everything. Select those issues that really matter to you. But don't have too many: a half a dozen issues will do! Then take your stand on them with clarity, confidence, and with courage - for the sake of the children.

#10   Cultivate the habit of speaking to children as people - people with minds - usually lively ones. Appeal to their good sense. It is not necessary to be sweet, silly or sentimental at one extreme, or somber, grim or harsh at the other. Let us be genuine, direct, honest, serious, and warm with them, and about them—and sometimes humorous too.

#11 The goal of education is not enjoyment; that is the goal of entertainment. As I have already suggested, the goal of education is to engage the minds of the learners so that their understandings of significant phenomena and events become deeper, clearer, and more accurate. When we succeed at engaging their minds in such things, they find it enjoyable. But, though enjoyment cannot be our main goal, it can be a by-product of good teaching.

#12 I really believe that we cannot have optimal environments for children in preschools, child care centers, and schools unless the environments are also optimal for the adults who work in them. Certainly on some days what is optimal for the children will be obtained at the expense of the adults (like Halloween parties), and on other days, vice versa. But on the average, on a day-to-day basis, both the children and the adults must find their lives together satisfying, interesting and worth living.

#13 Cultivate your own intellect and nourish the life of your own mind. For teachers, the cultivation of our minds is as important as the cultivation of our capacities for understanding, compassion and caring - not less, not more - but equally important. In other words, see yourself as a developing professional; become a student of your own teaching -- a career-long student of your own teaching.

#14 Respect your adversaries and resist the temptation to be defensive. Remember, whenever you respond defensively it is partly because you believe the attack, or believe part of the attack; and when you are defensive you are responding to the attacker's rules! Sometimes the attacker is right. But it seems best to respond professionally rather than personally. Furthermore, it seems to me that adversaries and enemies tend to become alike!

#15 Never take someone else's views or opinions of you or your work more seriously than you take your own! Take others' views seriously – there may be much to learn from them - but not more seriously than you take your own; for that is the essence of self-respect, and I believe that children benefit from being around self-respecting adults.

#16   Always assume that the people you work with have the capacities for greatness, creativity, courage and insight. Occasionally this assumption will be wrong, perhaps. But if you always make it, you will be much more likely to uncover, encourage, strengthen, and support these qualities in them.

#17   Never underestimate the power of ideas! Bad ones as well as good ones! Ideas are distinctly human creations, and if they were not powerful, many people would not have been imprisoned, exiled, assassinated, sent to Siberia, burned at the stake, or crucified - because of their ideas.

#18   I think the great struggle of our time - and no doubt for generations to come - is the struggle for equality. But we might ask: equality of what? People are not equally tall or musical or mathematical or athletic or beautiful; but they are equally human! They are equally human in the sense that they all have hopes, and dreams and wishes and fantasies and aspirations and fears and doubts. They all want to be treated with respect and dignity and want to feel loved by someone. In these ways it seems to me, all of the world's people have much more in common than they have apart!

#19   I have tried to share my own views of what education is about. To me it is about developing in the young certain dispositions. These dispositions should include being reflective, inquisitive, inventive, resourceful, full of wonder (wonder-full?), and perhaps puzzlement too. These dispositions should also include the habits of searching for evidence; they should also include the dispositions to be tender, courageous, caring, compassionate and include some humor as well! But I refer you to the definition of education provided by the British philosopher R. S. Peters:

> To be educated is not to have arrived at a destination; it is to travel with a different view. What is required is not feverish preparation for something that lies ahead, but to work with a precision, passion and taste at worthwhile things that lie at hand (Peters, 1965, p. 110).

#20.   I believe the time has come to redirect the goals of education away from the emphasis on producing rocket scientists to compete in the global economy. Instead, it seems to me the main goal of education should be to do whatever we can to help every child to grow to become a productive participant in his or her community and to be able to lead a satisfying life, whatever his or her occupation might be. To realize this goal we must be sure to emphasize the arts as well as other kinds of learning.

#21   I really believe also that each of us must come to care about everyone else's children. We must come to see that the well-being of our own individual children is intimately linked to the well-being of all other people's children. After all, when one of our own children needs life-saving surgery, someone else's child will perform it; when one of our own children is threatened or harmed by violence on the streets, someone else's child will inflict it. The good life for our own children can only be secured if it is also secured for all other people's children. But to worry about all other people's children is not just a practical or strategic matter; it is a moral and ethical one: to strive for the well-being of all other people's children is also right.

Part IV. Respecting the Learner[3]

One of the essential attributes of a good teacher —from preschool through to graduate school—is the disposition to respect learners. The concept of *respect* is an elusive one and is very difficult to define. But it is one of those elements of human relationships that we seem to know when we see it and when we feel it.

I suggest that to respect the learner means, among other things, attributing to the learner positive qualities, intentions, and expectations, even when the available evidence may cast doubts on the learner's possession of these attributes. A respectful relationship between the teacher and the learner is marked also by treating learners with dignity, listening closely and attentively to what the learners say, as well as looking for what they seem reluctant to say. Respect also includes treating the learners as sensible persons, even though that assumption sometimes requires a stretch of the teacher's imagination. When it comes to young children this element of respect implies that we should resist the temptation to talk to young children in silly sweet voices, heaping empty praise on them, and giving them certificates indicating that a smiling bear believes they are special. This disrespectful strategy makes a mockery of teaching. After all, teaching is about helping learners to make better, deeper, and fuller sense of their experience and to derive deep satisfaction from the processes of doing so. Education, after all, is not about amusement, excitement, or entertainment.

Respectful teaching conveys through the relationship between the teacher and the learner, confidence in the child's potential ability to overcome difficulties and to persist in the face of some inevitable obstacles. A respectful teacher is one who helps learners – of every age - who have persisted in the face of setbacks and reverses to accept their limitations gracefully and to be satisfied and gratified that they have done their very best.

---

3   An earlier version of this brief piece was written for inclusion on the State of Illinois Newletter called "Inside the Gateways," June 2006 Issue. <illgateways.com>

A respectful teacher is also one who helps students, even the young ones, to evaluate their own accomplishments as they progress, not in terms of whether their work is good or bad, or right or wrong, but in terms of other criteria they can gradually develop the habit of using. For example, you can ask in a serious and respectful way, "Is the drawing as complete as you want it to be?" or "Does the story you wrote (or told) include as much detail as you think it should or could?" Even preschoolers have been observed to respond to such appropriate queries thoughtfully and to indicate the beginning of a lifelong disposition to evaluate their own efforts thoughtfully.

Along similar lines, another important aspect of respectfulness in teacher–learner relationships is honesty. Teachers are often so eager to encourage children by praising them that after a while they develop the habit of issuing streams of empty and false praise that many children begin to dismiss as the inevitable, useless, and boring response of a kind and well-meaning teacher. Being honest when evaluating a student's work does not imply any kind of insulting or humiliating response to a child's efforts. Rather it implies conveying in dignified and serious tones how a piece of work or other kind of effort might have been better on relevant criteria, or could be improved in specific ways, or even redone. A teacher can often reassure a child by suggesting that he or she give the story or poem or picture another try, perhaps emphasizing or explaining that others will be more able to understand or enjoy the story or poem when the suggested revisions are made.

Another major element of respectfulness in professional behavior is the disposition to treat all of those we serve with dignity, even when we disagree with them, or even perhaps dislike them. To respect, accept, and treat with dignity a child or colleague or parent we like, enjoy, and agree with, is easy. We all can do that without much trouble. But it takes a true professional to be respectful and accepting of a child you might wish was absent from the class or meetings more often! To be a professional also means treating with dignity and acceptance parents and other adults we might dislike or with whom we disagree. After all, parents are just like people! Some are easier to develop relationships with than others.

Respect cannot be enacted or conveyed by gestures, trick phrases, or any other phony technique. It can only be communicated when the teacher's feelings toward learners are based on the deeply and profoundly held assumption that all humans are created equal—not equally tall, or equally mathematical, or equally athletic, musical, poetic, or on numerous other attributes. But we are all equally human in that we all have dreams, hopes, wishes, fears, and fantasies, and we all want and deserve to be treated with dignity and respect.

Part V. Stephen's Song Album[4]

Stories Behind the Songs

The Family Album is a collection of music that has been inspired directly or indirectly by my family. Some songs were written for specific family members. Others were written in response to relationships with individuals or groups outside the family. A few were created while teaching or in my studio, and are particularly close to my heart.

Track 1. I wrote the lyrics for the song **Father, Father** while my parents were overseas together, leaving us three at home for the first time. Each verse reflects how I feel about my immediate family members, and also my feelings of connection to all people.

Track 2. **Ballad of Boris** was written for my Father's 75th birthday celebration and family reunion. I recall how he exploded with laughter upon comprehending the songs' punch line. At his 80 birthday party I presented him with the recorded version of the Ballad of Boris on a portable CD player. This time he reacted with confusion and seemed not to remember the song at all. At the time I felt disappointed that, even with music, I could not reach through his increasing Parkinson's "haze". The experience helped me come to terms with just how far down the disease had taken him, and made me wonder how much longer he would be with us. At his funeral five months later, I sang the song and changed the ending to "We love you Dad, and we always will"

The opening line of the song reflects the fact that my father was born in Moscow, USSR. His parents decided to flee when he was about eight-years-old. Having no passports, the only city they could live in at that time was Shanghai, China where he lived until he was twenty-six-years old when he moved to the University of California in Berkeley, California.

---

4 Stephen is composer and performer of tracks 1-10 except where indicated. Tracks 1,4 and 8 appear on *First Person Singular*. Tracks 7 and 10 appear on *Looking Up*. Tracks 11 and 12 were created by Miriam and Bill Millikin.

Track 3. I wrote **Star In My Universe** the night before a date with the daughter of one of my mother's colleagues. I was intrigued by the young woman when we were introduced a week earlier, and through this song fragment I wondered who she might turn out to be. On our first and only date, we discovered that we had just one trait in common: a pronounced ability to maintain awkward silences. I cannot imagine a better sonic representation of our shared sense of remoteness than the strains of a radio broadcast at the beginning of this track. They were not added for effect, but came through the circuitry of my old tape deck, which also functioned, inadvertently, as a shortwave radio receiver.

Track 4. Until I wrote **Perfect Person**, words and music had always fallen together without much effort. But as a High School senior I struggled with the question of what was worth singing about. I answered by voicing some of the self-conscious thoughts and feelings that jangled around inside me. As lyrics emerged I thought, "I can't sing about that! Not only would I be embarrassed, but my audience might be, too." I wished that somebody else would sing this song, then concluded it was up to me to do it. When audiences responded enthusiastically, my thoughts and feelings jangled around a little less self-consciously. My mother expressed her appreciation for the song when she first heard it, but she did not hesitate to add that it didn't have much of a melody.

A note about the last line: By the time I recorded *Perfect Person* I was living in a small northwest Connecticut town where the population doubled (and income bracket shot through the roof) on weekends and holidays due the large number of second homes in the area. As a self-employed performer, composer and music teacher living hand-to-mouth, I often felt out of place there, and ached for a near future when I would live and work in a community of like-hearted artists. For the time being, I was able to laugh at my predicament by singing, in the final chorus, the words, "…I'll forget that I'm not the perfect person…", and, "…living in Washington, CT, of course."

Track 5. I wrote **Is That All Ya Know?** as a protest song. As a High School student, I sought to voice my disappointment in my teachers and many of my schoolmates for apparently opting for "conventional inner lives". Of course, I only had knowledge of my own inner life, which was just beginning to be my favorite subject. Most of what I knew about others, I learned with my friends and at home with family. If I felt disappointment about family or friends, I didn't dwell on it.

The song also asks whether the subjects of my protest had swallowed the "True Solution". I imagined this "drink" to be an antidote to creative growing pains which could restore the afflicted to a default setting of Institutional Expediency (when one carries the question, into new situations, "Is this going to be on the test?")

Track 6. The song **Entwining Family** was written for and performed at the wedding of my sister Miriam and her husband Bill. I finished music and lyrics the day before the ceremony at our home in Urbana, Illinois. My father was concerned that the song sounded too sad for the occasion of a wedding. I understood his point, but had a gut feeling about the appropriateness of the musical choices I had already made. (Besides, it was a little late to start from scratch.) Miriam was the first Katz child to marry, and the first one to alter a heretofore family five-ness. I wanted to express both the loss and the gain this occasion represented to me. In the end, my father's reaction inspired me to use the words, "Now it is time to say goodbye", and "... to say hello".

Track 7. **Bitterroot Prelude** is the unaccompanied first section of a larger work entitled Bitterroot Suite. Ten years in the making, the Prelude evolved as an *etude,* or practice piece in response to my fascination with a wide range of technical and musical challenges for the plucked, strummed cello. Early versions resembled some of the contrapuntal, chordal strumming patterns I tinkered with many years earlier on the guitar. As I mastered a particular pattern on the cello, a slightly more nuanced variation would suggest itself. After many iterations of this process, the suggestions ceased, and the piece was complete.

Track 8. I dedicated **Life Is More Than A Dream** to Aaron Millikin, Miriam's first child. He is also the first Katz grandchild, and my first nephew. I was thinking about the song *Row, Row, Row Your Boat*, which ends with the words, "… life is but a dream." I wanted to tell Aaron (who was still in the womb when I wrote this song) how I felt about life, things, and dreams: that our experiences while dreaming and awake are sublimely, symbolically linked.

It is hugely symbolic that this song concludes with the voice of my father shouting "You're on your own!" I prompted him to record this sound bite in 1990 to represent the exact words and tone he used when helping me learn to ride a bike as a kid. After getting me up to speed by pushing on the back of my seat, he would shout the line when he wanted me to know that he had let go, and that I was, indeed, on my own.

Frances Harmeyer, flute; Connecticut Conservatory Singers; Musical quote at 3:10 is from the Prelude of J. S. Bach's G Major Cello Suite.

Track 9. I composed **Cellophants** for beginning cellists with help from my young student Jenny V. during our lessons at the Connecticut Conservatory of Dance and Music in New Milford, Connecticut.(See Part VI for the poem I wrote to her as a final evaluation). The subtitle, "For a herd of young cellos" reflects my impression that cellos sound a lot like a elephants when playing together in large groups. The piece challenges cellists to use "extended techniques", e.g., bowing under the strings, left-hand pizzicato, harmonics, and something I call Cellophant Trunkations, which are designed to tame the kids who inevitably try to wield their bows at one another as if they were swords. You can hear them (gently!) thwacking their bows together towards the end of the piece.

This recorded performance was made at the final concert during a cello workshop weekend in Ann Arbor, Michigan in February 2005. The day after teaching the workshop I flew to Urbana, Illinois to attend my father's funeral.

Track 10. The original version of **Eight Days Of Eve** was one of many nameless cello improvisations on an old worktape until my wife Beth asked me to create a sound track for a video animation project titled "Eight Days of Eve". If not for her suggestion that I expand the sketch and include it in the score, I might never have shaped into the piece as it appears on this CD.

Track 11. **Small Stuff** was improvised using looping electronics with an echo effect. Percussion sounds were added later.

Stephen's Bio

Stephen is a cellist, guitarist, vocalist, and award winning composer. He premiered his cello compositions at Carnegie Recital Hall and performs frequently with the Paul Winter Consort. His repertoire of cello solo and ensemble compositions are studied and performed by cellists around the globe.

Stephen has worked extensively with dancers and choreographers, and has collaborated and performed with members of Pilobolus Dance Company, and has been a Visiting Artist at Amherst College. As a co-founder of the cello/movement/theater company Seen & Heard with the late dancer and monologist BJ Goodwin, he literally danced with the cello while accompanying the dramas they played out on stage.

Stephen's score for the documentary film The Rich Have Their Own Photographers won the Jury Prize Gold Medal for Best Impact of Music in a Documentary at the 2007 Park City Film Music Festival. His solo recording First Person Singular features his songwriting, singing and guitar playing in addition to the cello, and was hailed by Connecticut Songsmith as "an incredible debut album by a new and important artist". His recent releases, Looking Up and Earthdance feature his looped compositions and improvisations. (Available through iTunes and cdbaby.com)

A native of San Francisco, Stephen received a Master of Music degree from the Cincinnati College-Conservatory of Music, and lives in Haydenville, Massachusetts with his wife Beth and son Olin. skatz@cellocelli.com

Miriam's Album Notes

Track 12. **What Does the Season Mean?** It was the first week of December in 1996. Bill and I were cleaning up after dinner one night, and got to talking about the holiday season and how it had gotten completely out of hand. A time of year that was supposed to be joyous and meaningful seemed to be the exact opposite. Everyone is rushing around, shopping to the point of exhaustion, physically and financially. We both recalled how, as kids, for him with Christmas, and me with Chanukah, there was a true feeling of wonder and excitement that was now long gone. Was our inner child still buried underneath somewhere? That was the question which inspired the song, "What Does the Season Mean?" Bill, an accomplished musician, writer and producer headed into our studio that night and wrote the music, and I joined him to write the lyrics. Bill and I sang all of the vocals except for one verse sung by our oldest child, Aaron, then eight. The song was produced within a couple of days.

At that time, Bill was Creative Services Director for Clear Channel Communications overseeing imaging and commercial production for several radio stations here in Cincinnati. He presented "What Does the Season Mean?" to his general manager, who decided to put the song on the air that holiday season and many more after. At the same time, the local CBS TV affiliate, whom Bill worked also with regularly, heard the song, and decided to use it for their imaging promos throughout the holiday season.

Track 13. **Aaron's Goodbye**. This instrumental was written and produced my husband, Bill, the day after returning home from dropping off our oldest son at the University of Toledo, where he was to begin his freshman year. Our final glimpse of Aaron as we left was an emotional one. . . him trudging up a hill by himself, heading towards yet another late summer drumline practice with several dozen complete strangers. While Bill and I were choked up at seeing our oldest walking into a "new life", we were also aware of what possibilities lay ahead. The emotions felt when hearing this piece reflect how Bill and I felt that day.

Miriam Millikin's Bio

Miriam is a professional voiceover talent, singer and writer. She and her husband, Bill, own and run Creative Mills, a full service audio production company from their home-based studios in Cincinnati, Ohio. They spend their workdays writing and producing commercial jingles, radio ads, original music and voiceovers, and can be heard everywhere – from Champion Windows and Applebee's ads to narrations for MetLife, United, Lockheed-Martin and many others. Samples of their work can be found on their website, www.creativemills.com

Though most of Miriam's writing these days consists of advertising copy and lyrics, she has written pieces that have been published locally in the Cincinnati Enquirer and All About Kids magazine.

Miriam and Bill have three children, Aaron, Charlie and Sarah, as well as three dogs and three birds.

List of Songs on the Family Album[5]

	Creation date/recording date
Father, Father	1978/1991
Ballad of Boris	1998
Star in My Universe	1979
Perfect Person	1975/1991
Is That All You Know?	1976
Entwining Family	1982
Bitterroot Prelude	2002
Life Is More Than A Dream	1988/1991
Cellophants	1991/2005
Eight Days Of Eve	1998
Small Stuff	2007
What Does The Season Mean?	1996
Aaron's Goodbye	2007

---

5   Stephen is composer and performer of tracks 1-11 except where indicated. Tracks 1,4 and 8 appear on *First Person Singular*. Tracks 7 and 10 appear on *Looking Up*. All songs copyright Stephen Katz, 2008.

Tracks 12 and 13 were composed, performed, and recorded by Miriam and Bill Millikin.

1. **Father, Father** 4:08

Father, father, father me
Help me set my sails as far as I can see
Mother, mother, mother me
Help me when the winds of time appear to be
Appear to be stronger than the strength I feel inside of me
Appear to be stronger than the strength I feel inside.

Brother, brother, sail with me
Look upon the stars to guide us faithfully
Sister, sister, see the shore
After all we turn to land once more
And with an anchor to the rock of our new found land
We are a family one step closer to our home

2. **Ballad of Boris** 1:43

Born in Mother Russia, raised in Shanghai
With a passion for the piano and a glimmer in your eye
You made it to the melting pot through the Golden Gate
Where you met your bride-to-be and where you sealed yor fate

First came Daniel, then came Steve
Then came Miriam and the circle was complete

We're so glad you're our Dad
When we're down you make us sunny
When we're up you get so punny
When we're broke you send us...

Your love, your love, your love
We love you Dad
Happy birthday to you
(And many more)

3. **Star In My Universe** 1:11

Star in my universe
How do you shine
In my universe?

4. **Perfect Person** 3:27

I care so much about how I look
Sometimes I think:
if you don't like the cover you might not buy the book

I care so much about how I act
I'm an undercover playwrite as a matter of fact

You see, I'm not the perfect person that I someday hope to be
Meanwhile I simply seem to worsten, living in...
I don't know, some sort of self-indulgent, post-modern, abstract,
teenage purgatory

I think so much about who I want to be
I'm afraid to say, "I think I'm already me"
I think so much about what I say
Sooner or later I got to win at one of these word games I play
You see, I'm not the perfect person that I someday hope to be
Meanwhile I simply seem to worsten, living in...
I don't know, you tell me

I think so much about how I think
I wanna pull the plug and watch the kitchen sink
Mirror, mirror in my head, how can you cope with
all the sh** you're fed?

I hear ya tell me "Some day soon you got to pull yourself together.
As a perfect person you'll feel so much better"
You say, time will fly, and so will I, 'cause by and by, I'll forget that...

I'm not the perfect person that I someday hope to be
Meanwhile I simply seem to worsen, living in...
Washington, CT of course.

5. **Is That All Ya Know?** 2:00

Is that all ya know?
Is that all ya think?
It's all ya show
Enough to make one
Drink down the *True Solution*
Have you tried them all yet?
I can't tell

I can't tell if that's all ya know
Is that all ya say?
It's enough to make one
Drink down the *True Solution*

6. **Entwining Family** 3:30

Obvious though it may be
I have never told you
Miriam, my sister
Did you know, I love you

Now it is time to say goodbye
That is to say, you are, today
Wedding William

Now it is time to say hello
Brother, sister
Sons and daughters
Fathers, Mothers
Entwining family

Obvious though it may be
We are gathered here to say
All our love is with you now
And always
We love you
We love you
We do

7. **Bitterroot Prelude** 3:16

Recorded in concert, New Directions Cello Festival, Storrs, CT

8. **Life Is More Than A Dream** 3:54

Things are more than they seem
Life is more than a dream

I love you, I love you, I lo lo lo love you
I hug you, I hug you, I hu, hu, hug you
I kiss you, I kiss you, I ki, ki, kiss you

[Boris Katz shouts] You're on your own!

9. **Cellophants** (For a herd of cellos) 2:56

Cellocelli Workshop, Ann Arbor, Michigan

10. **Eight Days Of Eve** 6:33

Recorded at Signature Sounds, Palmer, MA

11. **Small Stuff** 4:00

12. **What Does the Season Mean?** 2:50

Its that time of year again and your list of things to do. . .
Just seems so overwhelming,
You don't know how you'll make it through,
But as you take the moment to search for Christmas joy,
Turn to the child inside. . .
What does the season mean to you?

Take away the tinsel, and the spirit will remain,
In the hearts of helpful strangers, or a caroler's refrain.
Now look at all your treasures and hold them as a gift,
Bring back the child inside
(Bring back the child)
What does the season mean to you?

What does the season. . .
What does the season. . .
(Cincinnati)
What does the season mean?

What does the season. . .
What does the season. . .
What does the season mean?

And if you think you have no treasures,
Look at all the ones you love. . .
There is a child inside. . .
(That's what the season means)
That's what the season means

Cincinnati celebrate!
All along the river share the day
Cincinnati celebrate, celebrate

Cincinnati celebrate!

What does the season. . .
What does the season. . .
What does the season mean?
(Chorus out)

13. **Aaron's Goodbye** 1:34

VI. Family Memorabilia

I have included these photos and poems and memorabilia of various kinds to help readers to appreciate the rich context in which I learned so much about parenting and teaching. These items also indicate well how own children constantly played with words, just like their wonderful father.

My twin sister and I in London, England, at about three-years-old. I am on the right.

&

My twin and I with our Mother at about the age of eight. I am on the left side.

Dear Mama—

I still remember
the very first thing
you ever taught me...

what it feels like
to be loved.

Happy Birthday!

With love
from Steve

6/7/04

I gave Steve this photograph of me holding him when he was about nine months old. Steve later used this photograph to create a birthday greeting that he sent to me in 2004.

father, father
father me
help me set my
sails as far as
i can see.
mother, mother
mother me
help me when the
winds of time
appear to be,
stronger than the
strength i feel
inside of me . . .

But who is this
who knows that i'm
as far as I set out to see,
as strong as I decide to be,
as long as I live up to me?

Steve, July 13, 1978

I found this beginning of a poem he later extended when my husband and I returned from our first visit to the People's Republic of China in 1978. It was the first time my husband and I had ever left our town, our country and left the three children without one of us nearby (they were 21,20 and 19 years-old at the time). The poem was later lengthened and forms the lyrics of one of the songs on the compact disc titled "Father, father." The additional versus can be seen in the lyrics on page 60.

an easy stare
out your window
from your chair
to watch the snow blow
at your scarf and at your face
and as your viewing is displaced
close your eyes and
softly say
mother's ties
still today hold
gems unpolished
tightly turning
rest between
the rapid brushing
knowing days of
when they come
from now will be
the precious ones
will always be
the precious ones

the precious ones
will always be
the precious ones
from now will be
when they come
knowing days of
the rapid brushing
rest between
tightly turning
gems unpolished
still today hold
mother's ties
softly say
close your eyes and
as your viewing is displaced
at your scarf and at your face
to watch the snow blow
from your chair
out your window
an easy stare

to with from steve dec. 21, 1977

A poem Steve left on my desk at my office in 1977. He wrote it while he was looking out of the window toward the parking lot waiting my return to the office so that he could borrow my car.

. . . and if, as my mother recently suggested to me, I <u>do</u> have constipation of the mind, I'm in favor of "Nature's Own Remedies" all the more. Rather than swallow the syrup of institutional expediency to flush out the appropriate letter grades, I prefer to sort through the bulk of my experiences, digest and absorb the parts thereof, (making neither haste nor waste), and excrete my findings in only the properest of places at only the properest of times.

Stephen Katz
July 24, 1977

When Steve was an undergraduate at the University of Illinois he took a required course in Rhetoric. He seemed to have great difficulty getting his writing assignments handed in on time. He seemed to suffer from some kind of "writer's block." Noting that pattern I accused him of suffering from mental constipation as he sat in front of blank paper for so long before getting anything written. This paragraph was written to his Rhetoric instructor and attached to an assigned paper that he handed in late, as usual.

> 25th Wedding
> Anniversary
>
> Dear Mom, dear Dad,
> your younger lad,
> is especially glad,
> for the years you've had.
> He knows you know,
> but wants to show,
> that it's as though,
> we're bound to grow,
> Among these nights
> to deeper hights
> upon these flights
> together.

A short poem Steve wrote to my husband and me on the occasion of our twenty-fifth wedding anniversary.

The three Katz children in 1977. Steve is 19 years-old and standing on the left. Dan is twenty years old and sitting on the right. Miriam is nineteen.

The entire Katz family in 1981, with Dan in the center.

3/23/83

Dear Mama,

 I trust that you are in the _very_ _best_ of optimal conditions, inside, if not out, seeing as how I have been sending huge amounts of love your way daily. And seeing as how I'm not the only one doing so.

 I feel you so close to me. When I think of you, you are here with me, just like when I needed you at school way back.

I love you,

Stephen

 The only letter that Steve wrote to me while I was a Fulbright Professor at the University of Baroda in India in 1983. However, he neglected to mail it to me and gave it to me upon my return home!

A photograph of Steve taken in the early eighties.

A photograph of Steve in an announcement of his recital in 1988 in the local newspaper.

THE O'HARE HILTON

Chicago, Nov. 18, 1983

My dear Steve,

As happens so often, once again my thoughts turned to you this morning — as, en route from Bismarck, N.D. to Chicago the flight took off into a splendid sunrise.

Sometimes my thoughts of you are quite mundane — will your car hold up a bit longer? Are you keeping warm this winter? Do you need new clothes, and other manifestations of a mother's ties! But most often the thoughts are not so easily phrased. I had just finished reading another wonderful novel by E.M. Forster — "A Room With a View". How could he write so insightfully about such ordinary people? About, as he says, those who "march to their destiny by catch-words" Or "life is a

P.O. Box 66414   Chicago, Illinois 60666   312/686-8000

A letter I wrote to Steve while I was traveling in 1983.

public performance on the violin, in which you must learn the instrument as you go along..."! And I sense again my own frustration at not having enough ways to express myself.

And I often think that there is much that you understand so quickly... and then wonder how well you are doing at husbanding your considerable gifts and whether you've accepted life's huge ambiguities, and whether you are creating music or drama or poetry and how you might react to something - a thought, or sounds, and how I'm looking forward to being in your company again.

And always when I'm teaching I'm reminded of how much I've learned from you.

There's more ofcourse.

I love you so.

Mama

(Letter continued)

&

MUSIC EVALUATION--MAY 1992
Student: Jenny Vogels   Teacher: Stephen Katz

Jenny, Jenny, Jenny,
What is left to say?
You bring joy to many
With every note you play

Here's a brief reminder
Which you may take along
To make your Maine move kinder
To sing your cello song:

Reach your left hand fingers boldly
Keep your left thumb right behind
Don't find high positions coldly
Just seek the sound you have in mind

Weren't too many hard facts, were there?
Regarding right hand things to know
But reach your nervous system further
Feel the string right through the bow

One last word on Art and Life
Not to take for granted--
Without Art we'd have no knife
To cut our ideas slanted

We'd have no playroom for our feelings
Attitudes would petrify
Our beliefs would catch us dealing
New creations on the sly

It's been said when we create
That we are playng God
But She plays us, well doesn't She?
It's not so very odd

Every artist uses art
To say what must be said
Here's to Jenny's good head start
Towards Art and Life ahead!

Music Evaluation. A poem Steve wrote in 1991 to one of his cello students as she prepared to move on to a new life in Maine.

4/9/08   77

All creators use their art
To say what must be said
Here's to Jenny's good head start
Towards Art and Life ahead!

****

Not all of my students at the Connecticut Conservatory of Dance
and Music received such poetic final evaluations from me. But since
Jenny and family were to relocate to Portland, Maine during the
following summer, I took the opportunity to express my
appreciation and affection toward this bright eyed eleven year old
with whom I shared so many key lesson over a two year period.

(Music evaluation continued)

&

CELLO MOVEMENT THEATER
BJ Goodwin *&* Stephen Katz

Photograph of Steve performing with the late B. J. Goodwin in 1996. Photograph taken buy Sally Cohn.

A photograph of me with my six grandchildren. On the grass are Dan and Beth's twins, from left to right: Noah and Jonah. Behind them from left to right are Miriam and William's three children: Aaron, Sarah and Charlie, and on my lap is Steve and Beth's nine-month-old Olin. This photograph was taken on the occasion of laying the stone on my husband Boris's grave in 2006.

Dear Dad

Birthday Greetings From Dan

A truly dear Dad you are

Center of my universe...the true superstar

From birth to now, you sure know how.

It began early as you "Russia-ed" to China

You escaped without a shiner

The sun shone bright as you crossed the Pacific

San Francisco sure was terrific.

You bridged the Golden Gate singing La, La, La[1]

Then you married her, Ha Ha Ha

Next came Dan, Steve and Mir,[2] one, two, three

We brightened your life, filled it with glee.

Mir had the fiddle, Steve used a bow

Dan tried clarinet, it made everyone go.

Dad with your slide rule, Mom with her "gift"

Through Willie Mays, Rocky[3], Fluffy

And litters of kitties we sift.

---

[1] La was a nickname given to me very early by my twin sister!

[2] Mir was the nickname for our daughter Miriam. It also means "peace" in Russian, her father's first language!

[3] Our dog, and Fluffy was the cat.

A poem written by Dan to his father for his birthday, probably when he was in his late seventies.

A move from the Bay to Urbana then follows,

For California natives a tough pill to swallow.

Then came the tweens with your litter of three

Thank goodness we'd already learned the ABCs

These were the tough years, not always the best

And we constantly put your good patience to the test

You tried urban planning as Mom trotted the globe

Always smiling while carrying the load.

You conquered all hurdles with compassion and care

If not the world, the family...swords to plowshares.

In the scheme of things we're a pretty good lot

Cysts and Parkinson's are almost forgot.

What a great man you are, my wonderful Dad

This son's the envy, and certainly glad.

I hope **my** beautiful sons look to me as if I'm a star

If I turn into half the father you are.

Happy Birthday Dad....I love you.

(Poem continued)

"The Story of My Mummy and Me." The first "book" written by my daughter Miriam when she was seven-and-a-half years old – a time when I was in my first year of doctoral studies. The actual "book" consists of three index cards and taped together to form a little book.

```
Dear Mom,

It's impossible to birthday shop for you, so I decided to look inward for
gifts.  Then, after I wrote this poem, I realized that the same sentiments
apply to Dad as well.  But...it's YOUR birthday, so PLEASE take it
personally!


                         Mom, you are to me
                     More than the sand is to the sea,
                   'Cause when I wash up on your shores
                     I leave stronger...standing solidly.

                       And Mom, despite the miles,
                   I see you even in my children's smiles,
                   'Cause your inherent love's resemblance
                     Lives here in your youngest child.

                   And though your birthdays come and go,
                   It's *your* gifts that always seem to grow,
                       At least that's how it feels to me...
                     Thank you Mom, for all you know!

                           I love you.
                      Happy 39th Birthday!

                             Miriam
```

A birthday greeting from Miriam to me. Probably sent to me in the early nineties.

Hi Mom,   1981

    Just a note from
your Mir dear...
Do you know that I
listen to you when I'm
away? That way I
always feel at home
wherever I am. Of course
it isn't actually you, but
it's common sense with
your voicebox — A vision
of you in my head and
I'm never misdirected
(But you're directly missed anyway)
           Love,
              Mir

    A note I found on my desk from Miriam in 1981 when she stopped in town briefly when she and her husband William were spending most of their time performing in a band around the country.

How To Survive Shopping With Children
By Miriam Millikin
10/01

It was late morning and the grocery aisles were vacant. The kids were in school. I came at a good time. Aah, peace in the produce section I thought, but my moment of zen ended abruptly as I rounded the corner into baked goods.

"Jimmy, get over here...NOW." Jimmy's mom had one hand on her hip, the other grasping a toddler teetering over the side of the grocery cart, and sweat beading up on her forehead. "And put that candy back where you found it, or no TV for the rest of the day!" Jimmy, like most four year olds, seemed to think this real-life adventure was worth missing out on Blue's Clues, because he was headed in the opposite direction.

Sound familiar? Is there a mom who hasn't been held hostage by her own children while shopping? I remember many trips to the grocery store interrupted by my attempts at discipline and ending in tears, sometimes my own. Now my kids are a little older, one of them is even old enough to baby sit the other two, so those days of tantrums in the checkout line are pretty much over. In case you haven't been through it yet with your child, let me just tell you, it's not one of those "cute phases." Oh, there will be an occasional sympathetic smile from fellow shoppers, as if to say, "I know you're having a hard time, and I've been there girlfriend, but right now I sure am glad I'm not you."

While that's not a problem, sometimes you will receive unsolicited advice. I'll never forget an in-store struggle I had with my oldest son when he was three. It was the typical, "No you can't have that..." followed by his high decibel reaction . An elderly woman nearby lifted her cane, waved it at my son and offered these words of wisdom: "Honey, what that child needs is a good whoopin'!" Though I was clearly frustrated, I knew a spanking was not going to solve anything. All normal children are curious,

A story Miriam wrote about the ordeal of shopping with a gang of young children.

and, think about it-- a grocery store is like 'Temptation Island' to a kid. Unfortunately, that means Mom is playing "Survivor".

So, now I'm the mom sans young kids, shopping under the speed limit, never again having to worry about Junior leaving his blankie back in aisle 9. I'm not trying to rub it in. You won't have to share your purse with a jelly stained Elmo forever. Before long, your only problem when you go to the store will be remembering where you parked your car when you come out. In the mean time, there are ways to make shopping with children easier--aside from leaving them with a babysitter, that is. Here are some tips to get you in and out with your temper intact:

Plan Ahead:

~Always make a shopping list. Get your children involved in the process. Have them check the refrigerator or pantry to see what you need to buy. Then, tell them you must stick to the list.

~If they ask for something special for themselves, and you think it's reasonable, put it on the list BEFORE you leave. This will lessen their demands for goodies while you're shopping.

~Shalie Schacht, a Cincinnati mother of three says, "I make sure my daughter has had her nap, and has on a fresh diaper" Don't take a cranky kid to the store.

~Feed your children (and yourself) before you go. You know how you always spend more on food when you're hungry? Imagine how your kids feel when the're looking at cookies and cakes on an empty stomach.

~Even if your children eat first, it's always a good idea to bring some snacks along. I'll admit, I've opened a box or two of crackers before getting to the checkout line, but I'm sure store management would prefer that I wait.

~For the very young ones, don't forget to pack some small, soft toys or books.

If A Meltdown Occurs:

There are times your child will cause a scene no matter what you do. When this happens, the key is to stay calm.

~Shalie says her two year old no longer wants to sit in the cart, and occasionally throws a fit. "First, I try to talk to her, but I stand my ground. I might give her a cookie-- but if she continues, sometimes I just leave the store." Shalie stresses the importance of teaching proper behavior in public.

~Laura Staubach, who has five children, agrees. "If you give in to their demands in the store, it's all over. You've lost control, and it will only get harder in the long run." So, if your child is screaming for 'Dunkaroo Lunchables', and you get them just to quiet her down, you're setting yourself up to be manipulated this way over and over again--in public, and at home.

Grocery Store Treasures and Traps:

~Shalie's 5 year old often uses one of the child-sized carts that are available in many stores. It's a great way to make small ones feel like they're doing something big.

~While Laura's children like the novelty and comfort of those large, double seated shopping carts, she has a complaint or two at the checkout line. "The lanes are too narrow, and there are so many things right there for my toddler to grab! Once she almost pulled a whole rack of batteries over." They're called "impulse" items for a reason.

The Mary Poppins Approach:

~ Most families go to the grocery store a least a couple of times a week, so it's not unusual to feel as if you're always 'dragging' the kids along. One way to change that, is to make it more of an investigation or a game. It takes only a little effort on your part, but your kids will learn a lot, and feel great because they're helping you.

~Starting with your shopping list, give children age-appropriate responsibilities. For example, getting items off of the shelves, or checking them off the list.

~If you have the luxury of time, have them compare or count the different types of breads, meats, cheeses, or even cookies. They might ask someone in the bakery

(Ordeal of shopping continued)

department how many cookies they bake in one day, or ask the butcher how they make ground beef. The possibilities are endless.

Obviously you don't want to have an all day field trip at the grocery store. One or two diversions are all you need to make shopping with children easier and surprisingly rewarding. And, when shopping goes smoothly, it always goes faster.

A Writer's Mother-Load

A sudden inspiration would be nice. . .
The perfect choice of words is worth any price
But what if every well is dry?
Will I ever be satisfied simply with the try?

And when the windfall comes,
I'm sure that I'll be ready
Should I expect profundities,
Or just a rhyme, say, like spaghetti?

There's potential deep inside somewhere,
It's there; I know I feel it,
But I also feel exhausted, mostly,
And sleep? I think I steal it!

If I could write instead of dreaming,
I'm sure I'd make my way,
But where I'd get, I'll never know,
So, I think, asleep I'll stay.

A poem titled "A Writer's Mother-Load" by Miriam K. Millikin

Becoming a Dog Lover
Miriam Millikin
(4/3/01)

When I was growing up we always had cats. Oh, we had a couple of dogs along the way, but when your last *name* is Katz, it just made sense that cats would rule. My brothers and I figured out that over the years we witnessed more than two-dozen litters of kittens being born. No, not by the same mother! One mother cat succeeded another. I don't remember what happened to each one of them, they probably ran away to find a family that would take them to the vet to have them sterilized. We always named the mother cat Fluffy, I suppose to honor her predecessor, and they would labor every spring and fall, teaching us, in living color, just how babies came into the world. It saved my parents some explaining, because we had a kid's eye view right into my bottom dresser drawer.

My brothers and I made projects out of entertaining the new kittens. We'd take huge moving boxes and create kitty playgrounds in them with strings hanging and cardboard cubbies and catnip balls. And though the mothers were always named Fluffy, we managed to get a little more creative, giving each kitten a different name. Okay, maybe not that creative, with names like Tiger or Boogar or Brownie or Spots, but to us they were all pretty special, which made giving them away very hard. Sometimes we would keep one from a litter, and her name would end up being...you guessed it, Fluffy. When the kittens were about six weeks old my Mom would put an ad in the paper; 'FREE KITTENS TO LOVING HOMES. CALL MRS. KATZ". Tell me, who, wanting a kitten would NOT respond to that ad? We never had a problem giving them away.

The dog was always an afterthought I'm sorry to say. One incident I clearly remember involved Rocky, our wirehair mutt who could run faster than anyone chasing him (usually my Dad, swearing the whole way!). Somehow my brother, Steve, who was about 8 at the time, got in between Rocky and Fluffy fighting

"Becoming a Dog Lover" A story about her gradual transformation from being a kitten lover as a child to becoming a dog-lover like her husband William.

like, well, cats and dogs. I guess only another 8 year old would know why he would try to break them up, but Steve ended up having a nice, big chunk of flesh torn out of his thigh. Soon after, Rocky got the ol' heave-ho, not through any fault of his own, more likely because he was simply outnumbered.

I met Sam about a year after I met my husband Bill. Bill and I were in a band together. He was the sax player and I was the "chick singer". For some reason Bill wanted to bring a little sanity to life on the road, so he adopted Sam, a one-year-old beagle mix with a questionable past. This was evident the very day Bill brought him home from the pound. Somewhere along his vagrant way Sam had contracted worms. And not the microscopic kind. In fact, they were evident for all the passers-by on that busy street corner to see. There was Bill, in the yard—with rush hour traffic force-fed the visual of a young man chasing after a dog in an attempt to help him expel tapeworms. Needless to say, Bill was already a dog lover.

Sam seemed to be a perfect fit for the rock and roll lifestyle. I'd bet over the next 8 years he marked more territory than Mick Jagger. Throughout those years we traveled across the country touring the 'not-so-classy club circuit'. Our lives consisted of driving, setting up equipment for a two or three week stint, playing dance music night after night, partying, sleeping, getting up late, working out, writing music or learning new cover songs, tearing down equipment and moving on to the next gig. And through it all Sam remained the center of our little universe. It was as if we were the couple with the child. The other band members would always gather in our room to hang out with "the family" since they were away from their own. I'm sure Sam had something to do with that congregation.

One night I remember returning to the band house to find that Sam had gotten into the cooler and eaten almost everything, including a couple of raw steaks! As the rest of the guys arrived, (in various states of consciousness) they saw

("Becoming a Dog Lover" continued)

&

us scolding Sammy for doing, in fact, what any normal dog would do if left alone with an UNLOCKED cooler. So, they joined in chanting, Sammy! Sammy! Sammy! Okay, so we were all young, stupid, and apparently cruel. And there was poor Sam, lying on the floor, guilt-ridden from his bloody chops to his tucked in tail. At first he was on his back and totally submissive, but when he couldn't take any more, in true rock and roll fashion, he ejaculated and scurried away.

Abuse was not the intention. We all loved Sam, and he changed *me*, a once "What's so great about dogs?" person, into someone writing about her own transformation. He was a nomad's best friend. On the road from Chicago to San Diego, then back to Illinois by way of Florida, it was certainly more of a dog's life than a human's. Stopping just long enough to define a memory, be it a flood in San Diego, a blizzard in the Rockies, or some idiot on the dance floor puking in front of the guitar player. Some things you just never forget.

We used to play somewhat regularly at a club in Merrilville Indiana. Where? That's what we said too, when our agent, Ted Pfeffer called us in Farmington, New Mexico to tell us we had to be there in 3 days. As it turned out, Merrilville was the home of the Holiday Star Theater, a fairly classy concert venue attached to a huge Holiday Inn and Holidome. Who would have thought we would meet the likes of James Taylor, Michael McDonald, Kenny Loggins and Lou Rawls (among others) in this paltry corner of Indiana? But that's another story. I don't think Sammy was impressed by all the celebrities. In fact, I remember him having at least a couple of bouts of intestinal flu during the course of our stays...but it was probably because, even though we gave him dog food, he pretty much ate what we ate. That's enough to make anyone sick. That was before he jumped off the roof.

The band rooms were in a newer section of the hotel on the third floor. Our room had one window that would open onto the flat gravelly roof of the original structure. It was a nice enough room, but you can bet James and Kenny and Michael's digs were in the other wing. However, it was perfect for Sam. When he needed to relieve himself, we'd just let him out the window. Once, when we came back to our room after rehearsal, Sam was gone. Since there was no place to hide in that 12 square foot room, we immediately suspected he had been stolen. Then we saw the window ajar. I crawled out to search the expansive roof beyond. Still, no Sam. It was very strange. After all, he was an obedient dog, but we never told him to take a flying leap! Unfortunately, that's exactly what happened, and surprisingly there's a happy ending. Our drummer, Don, found Sam wandering around outside the hotel, his chin (or whatever you call that part of a dog) scraped and bloody, but his tail wagging. Relief washed over our strange little family. We should have written a song about it.

("Becoming a Dog Lover" continued)

&

Anniversary Poem

Miriam Millikin
11/2/02

It was the two of you - combined by a glance
That day by the bay at an international dance,
And since then there've been fifty-years in between…
It's an American dream, why, what HAVEN'T you seen?
But more, so much more than your three little Katz
Life together has brought you, and these are the facts..,
While rearing your kittens, you too did grow,
Engineering and planning, educating just so…
And moves, there were moves, to make life much better,
After all, Stanford created Professor go-getter!
How could Katzes continue in San Mateo County
While mid-western cornfields called for their bounty?
It may not have compared to their Barbados cabana,
Still, Boris and La moved to Shampoo-Banana.
From 201, 503 to 2002,
Pick any address, each one they outgrew!
So the kittens went on to their own litter boxes…
At times moved back in, it was getting obnoxious,
But generally speaking they all settled down,
Dan literally became the talk of his town!
Stephen went eastward with guitar and cello,
And Mir wed a tall, very musical fellow.

Mom and Dad, looking back now at your first fifty years,
Sifting through smiles, sorting through tears,
Is a treasure so very few married know…
Anniversary: golden, with more jewels to go.

Happy 50th Anniversary to a couple of real gems,

Love,
Mir, Bill, Aaron, Charlie & Sarah

A poem Miriam sent to us on the occasion of our fiftieth wedding anniversary.

Notes